Purity in Progress™
A Frank Study of Faith & Relationships

DANIELLE HORNE

PURITY IN PROGRESS™

Over time not overnight.

Written by Danielle Horne

Black **rim**
M e d i a
& Publishing

BLACK RIM MEDIA & PUBLISHING, MORAGA, CA

Book cover designed by Danielle Horne derived from the following works:

ID 29739153 © Eyluleylul | Dreamstime.com

http://www.dreamstime.com/stock-photos-heart-devil-angel-symbols-isolated-white-high-quality-d-render-illustration-image29739153 #stockimages via @dreamstime

ID 12794761 © Natallia Hudyma | Dreamstime.com

http://www.dreamstime.com/stock-image-set-hearts-design-image12794761 #stockimages via @dreamstime

ID 4450419 © Qqibb| Dreamstime.com

https://www.dreamstime.com/royalty-free-stock-images-clip-art-broken-heart-needle-image4450419 #stockimages via @dreamstime

ISBN: 099794000X
ISBN-13: 978-0-9979400-0-8

PURITY IN PROGRESS™

© 2016 Danielle Horne, Moraga, CA

DEDICATION

This book is dedicated to YOU Reader. You came to this book looking for truth that was biblical, sexual, romantic, vulnerable and real. You are looking for a place you can face yourself and emerge with a stronger, wiser self. You are looking to understand what it means to be both sexual and sacred; to love, be loved and honor God with how you get love. If you are this person, this book is dedicated to you.

My Progression

Purity in Progress™ is a study in relationships from a biblical perspective. Over 20 years ago, I told God if he could do better with my romantic life than I was doing he could have it. It would take a few dating disappointments and a failed marriage before I let God lead me in this area. In the past ten years, I've learned about God's standard for love, his context for sex, and practical application of faith and celibacy. The precepts in this book come from the core teaching God gave me to share when I formed a women's Bible study years ago. If you're looking for answers beyond "pray about it" you can find them here.

CONTENTS

Acknowledgments   i

Chapter 1   The Playbook   1

Chapter 2   About God   4

Chapter 3   About You   9

Chapter 4   About Them   16

Chapter 5   About Your Body   24

Chapter 6   About Temptation   26

Chapter 7   About Honor   33

Chapter 8   About Sex   37

Chapter 9   About Love   51

Chapter 10   About Marriage   56

Chapter 11   Purity Plan   68

Chapter 12   Maintenance Plan   78

Chapter 13   Vision   80

Chapter 14   Resolution   82

ACKNOWLEDGMENTS

Thanks be to God for answering my questions about sex and intimacy!

Thanks to my parents, family, and friends for their love and support during the creation of this project.

And special thanks to Omar Lye-Fook, MBE of the UK. Over the course of four years, I lost many things. I ended up in a darkness I did not know how I would find my way out of. When I prayed, the only answer I got was a sound. That sound was the music of Omar which brought with it a light that got brighter each time I played it. I learned to "Sing (if you want it)" in my sorrow. God bless you and your family.

CHAPTER 1 – THE PLAYBOOK

A man's plan for a woman usually involves a mint and a condom and beyond this, he has no plan. He's operating on what's in his pocket. He's seeking her for "it." She's using "it" to get him. This is society's mating playbook. Eventually, you're supposed to "back into" the right person.

She's putting that thing on him. And even if she has his things she still doesn't have him. Fellas, God's design, is for the woman who gets you to be the woman who *gets you*. Ladies, God's design, is for the man who *gets* you to be the man who k*eeps* you. Using our methodology, we have the pleasure of pursuit, but not fulfillment. We keep pursuing the same things, the same way, ending up in the same place.

The disappointment I encountered prompted me to start from scratch. I had to look at the definitions, differences, and purposes between love and sex; the way I see my value, the way I see God, the way I view men, and how I envision sharing my life.

We think of sex as a right, but it is a privilege. To do God on God's terms, I have to define things and respect them the way he does. God has sheltered sex (meaning set it aside) for marriage. He put boundaries around it, but we just see sex as bound in a religious context. We seek to let it loose, to make it free. Free sex is costly and reveals our value, whether we want to admit it or not. We open our bodies to people that we wouldn't leave in our homes if we weren't there. Intimacy on any level risks exposure. God's design is for you to reveal yourself to someone who made a lifelong commitment to cover you.

I realized the method of dating and mating I was using pushed me further away from the life I wanted. I wanted to have a mate and a family, but I didn't know how to approach it in a God-honoring way. I didn't know how to get what I wanted and honor God at the same time.

The truth is the reason we struggle with sex is, God is on one side, and we are on the other. We cannot talk with God about this area because we don't agree with him. We agree with our fears, our desires, and our ego. When it comes to sex, these are our gods. **We struggle with God in this area because we do not trust him. You will only obey God to the degree you trust him.** You don't believe in God's Word if you are not trying to live it. Obeying the Word is a result of faith in God. That faith is a belief that God is who he says he is; God can do what he says he can do, and his instructions are the way to go.

In his book Visioneering, Andy Stanley writes, "Faith is not a power or force. It is not a vehicle by which we can coerce God into something against his will. It is simply an expression of confidence in the person and character of God. It is the proper response to the promise or revelation of God."[1]

THINK ON THESE THINGS

What do you believe? You need only to follow your actions to see what you believe. Saving money can't be important to you if you don't have a savings account you deposit into *regularly*. Saving time in the morning can't be important to you if you don't prepare the night before. You need only to follow your actions to see what you believe about yourself, love, sex and God. Let's look at a scenario. Imagine we have a phone with a late night seductive text message from a lover in one hand and the Bible in the other. For this scenario to be true, let's ask some questions to reveal the beliefs involved.

- Why are you only getting texts late at night? What makes that OK?

- This person is reaching out to you. What would happen if you didn't respond? Who says you have to?

When I host a relationship group, these are the types of questions I ask. The women who come to the group want to know more about practical application for godly living; discernment, boundaries, etc. This book is an overview. I can show you the mountain (what God has for us). Deciding to climb it (to live like you believe it) will be up to you. However, I strongly believe after seeing what God has for you; you'll be more than willing to climb the mountain.

CHAPTER 2 – ABOUT GOD

A good checkpoint to have when you are struggling in an area as a believer is your concept of God. Who is God?

Jesus is Lord

Many people who do not attend church or identify as Christian, consider themselves spiritual. Others believe Jesus was a good teacher, but are not Christ followers. They understand the commitment, but are not ready to make it. You cannot be a Christ follower and not be subject to his kingdom. If you seek to follow Christ, you are following a King, a ruler of his domain.

I love epic films covering tales of the ancient kings and kingdoms. One of my favorites is the movie, <u>Troy</u>. At one point in the movie, the King of Troy is sitting with his son Paris. The son recently stole the love of his life, Helen, from another king which puts the country on the brink of war. The King asks his son, "Do you love Helen?" Paris replies, "I love Helen like you love Troy." The King recounts his love for Troy, his vast and beautiful kingdom. The King says his love for Troy covers every blade of grass, every grain of sand, every rock. In the king's domain, everything is his, down to the last man, woman, child, beast, and crop. The citizens of the kingdom own nothing except what the king permits. The king's rule brings order and protects against lawlessness. The taxes paid to the king provide grain, seed, and protection for his people. As long as the king is not oppressive, he deserves allegiance. Citizens of the kingdom are also called subjects. As such, we are subject to the king's rule.

A part of the struggle we Christians have with our faith is that we do not want a king's rule. We want what we want, and we want God to be okay with it. This relationship sounds a lot more like a consultant. We give an offering and pay our tithes. We give our laundry list of prayers to God for him to meet, and hope he will see things our way. Are we following God or do we want him to follow us? Idolatry is when we try to make God in our image. God makes us in his image. God says, "You are mine, I have called you by name" (Isa. 43:1). We were bought with a price (I Cor. 6:18-19).

You can determine what you are following based on where you end up. If you end up somewhere that God did not want you to be (as revealed by his Word), chances are you did not follow him there. You followed something else. Not like I haven't done that before! When that happens, I usually end up in a place where I need God to get me out.

A Good Person

In a children's tale of wizardry and wonder, a young hero strolls through an attic and happens upon a mirror. Anyone who gazes into this mirror perceives they have received what they desire most. I was fascinated by the concept and thought about what my one wish would be. Do you know what your one wish is?

My wish was for the health and wholeness of my family. I was quite satisfied with this choice. Then I had an awful epiphany. The thing I desired most was not God. He should be. His fellowship, his presence, his will should be first. I am a Christian, and he is not first! I felt utterly undone. For God to truly be God to you, his place in your heart must be absolute. God's place in your heart should compete with nothing. I thought about why God was not in my mirror as my greatest desire. Anything I could want God could grant me so why wasn't he first? Could it be that I cannot control God? I cannot predict what he will do, when he will do it, and it might not be to my liking. I thought I was a "good" person!

Now, I sit in the truth of who I am. God is not first, but he should be. Even at our best, we somehow keep God small. Look at the distance between my heart and God's. This is fallenness. This is sin. Look at how high he is. Look at this gap. How can I close it? I can't close it, but I know who can. Jesus. He is my Savior. The sacrifice he made, his grace and truth not only bridges the gap, but leads me on a path to grow a heart that pleases God; a heart that seeks to put God first. He is not just Savior in the next life, in eternity. He is Savior now, in this life.

You can be a good person. You can want good things, but that is not the same as following God through Jesus. One soul says, "Hey, I'm doing the best I can. Jesus, you gotta help me." The other soul says, "God, what do I need you for?" Both souls struggle. The question is, what direction are you pulling in? I need Jesus. His example, the Word, and the Holy Spirit grow in me the hope of reflecting him by fulfilling my purpose in a way that pleases God. This God concept says God is a redeemer, a healer, not my accuser and someone who wants the best for me.

As Gary Thomas notes in his book <u>Sacred Marriage</u>, "The righteousness God seeks is persistent righteousness, a commitment to continue to make the right decision even when, perhaps hourly, you feel pulled in the opposite direction. Holiness is more than an inclination toward occasional acts of kindness and charity. It is a commitment to persistent surrender before God. Persistence doesn't make sense unless we live with a keen sense of eternity."[2]

Recap

This book is about purity so why am I starting with this God concept stuff? As you can see, your perspective on God's motives and his character toward you will either lead or mislead you in what you do. The tension we live in as Christians is, "Do I even *want* to obey God? If I do, do I have the ability?" I cannot answer the first question for you. You must search yourself to find that out. This book is dedicated to answering the second question. You have the God-given ability to obey him. You do not have to try to obey him on your own. God is with you. He will help you obey him if you ask. **Since God has called you to live holy, he has empowered you by the Holy Spirit to do so.** This is the will of God, even your sanctification, that you should abstain from fornication (sexual immorality), that each one of you should know how to possess your vessel in sanctification and honor (1 Thes. 4:3–4). God has given us all things that pertain to life and godliness (2 Pet. 1:3). You can do all things through

Christ who strengthens you (Phil. 4:13). You have what you need. We're going to look at how to put it together.

Why Don't We Obey God?

On the surface, it appears we don't obey God because of our inabilities and self-perceptions. Underneath we find out, we don't obey God because we cannot control him. You'll be challenged to relinquish your control to follow God. Another facet that will waiver is our view of God. Our default thinking is that someone is withholding something from us or that God is mean-spirited. We regularly read his Word to remind us how he defines himself. We will only obey God to the degree we trust him. Once we lose accurate perspective of who God is, obeying him is harder to do.

In his book, The Radical Disciple, John Stott notes, "Nearly all our failures stem from the ease with which we forget our comprehensive identity as disciples."[3] Not only do we get in trouble when we forget *who* we are, we also need to remember WHOSE we are. Stott continues, "Our common way of avoiding radical discipleship is to be selective: choosing those areas in which commitment suits us and staying away from those areas in which it will be costly. But because Jesus is Lord, we have no right to pick and choose the areas in which we will submit to his authority."[4]

God is our maker. He is God. We are his. Purity is not just about celibacy; it is about totally belonging to God, yielding to his authority, trusting his wisdom and submitting to it. In America, we have a traffic sign in the shape of a yellow triangle labeled "yield." In the United Kingdom, the yellow triangle is labeled, "give way." We struggle with God because we are trying to lead him rather than allowing him to lead us. We do not give way. In the same seemingly helpless, unfolding yieldedness with which we succumb to pleasure, we must learn to let God lead us into to pleasing him. We must give way.

THINK ON THESE THINGS

We are living for God. He is not living for us. We are made in God's image. When we try to make God in our image, we make God small. We make an idol. Consider the following:

- Is your perception of God based on who he says he is in his Word or something else?

- Who are you following, God or you?

- Do you trust him with your intimacy? Why or why not?

CHAPTER 3 – ABOUT YOU

I wrote this book to raise God consciousness more than sin consciousness. I could scare you with Scripture here. Whatever action not done out of faith is sin (Rom. 14:23). Oops, you just doubted. Well, you just sinned. If you want an overview of sin in this age, let's look at 2 Timothy chapter 3.

> But realize this, that in the last days difficult times will come. For men will be lovers of self, lovers of money, boastful, arrogant, revilers, disobedient to parents, ungrateful, unholy, unloving, irreconcilable, malicious gossips, without self-control, brutal, haters of good, treacherous, reckless, conceited, lovers of pleasure rather than lovers of God, holding to a form of godliness, although they have denied its power; Avoid such men as these.

> 2 Timothy 3:1-5 (NASB)

We sin when we are arrogant, ungrateful or can't celebrate the good that happens to others. We also sin when we don't get enough sleep or eat properly. With all this sinning, it's amazing we can live right at all!

We can live a life that pleases God, but first, we have to let God be God in our everyday lives. The King James translation of Scripture for this passage lists, "… lovers of pleasure **more than** lovers of God." I see this as an algebraic expression.

Lovers of pleasure > lovers of God

Paul was writing about people who called themselves Christians. By their admission, they love God, but they love something else more. What could be more than or greater than God?

The expression could also be read this way.

$$God < Pleasure$$

God is less than pleasure. What is God less than?

Let's say we love pleasure just as much as God. The expression would look like this:

$$Pleasure \geq God$$

Pleasure is greater than or equal to God. That would still be a false statement because there is NOTHING equal to God! NO THING is equal to God (Heb. 6:13). That's what makes him God.

Sin inaccurately depicts God. It makes untrue statements about God that directly oppose his nature and character.

I called the previous algebraic statements, expressions, but they are also equations. The difference between an expression and an equation is the equation has a solution.[5]

Solution - The Power of Godliness

Paul continues to speak of these Christians who love something more than God. He says they have a form of godliness, but deny the power thereof. We want to remain in control. If we are ordering God around, is he God or are we God? Between the two of us, which one of us is more qualified for God's job? The power of godliness cannot be activated in our lives if we have an idol (something we love more) in God's place. The solution to this equation involves us being willing to pull down our idols and allow godliness to have its power in our lives.

God Knows My Heart

Indeed, God does know your heart. Let's look at that thought through the story of Abraham and Abimelech:

And Abraham journeyed from thence toward the south country, and dwelled between Kadesh and Shur, and sojourned in Gerar. And Abraham said of Sarah, his wife, She is my sister: and Abimelech king of Gerar sent, and took Sarah. But God came to Abimelech in a dream by night, and said to him, Behold, thou art but a dead man, for the woman which thou hast taken; for she is a man's wife. But Abimelech had not come near her: and he said, Lord, wilt thou slay also a righteous nation? Said he not unto me, She is my sister? And she, even she herself said, He is my brother: in the integrity of my heart and innocency of my hands have I done this. And God said unto him in a dream, Yea, I know that thou didst this in the integrity of thy heart; for I also withheld thee from sinning against me: therefore suffered I thee not to touch her. Now, therefore, restore the man his wife; for he is a prophet, and he shall pray for thee, and thou shalt live: and if thou restore her not, know thou that thou shalt surely die, thou, and all that are thine.

Genesis 20:1-7 (KJV)

God knew the heart of Abimelech. God saw two desires in Abimelech. God saw the desire within Abimelech, which drove him to take Sarah into his palace. Abimelech had clear romantic intentions for Sarah. God also saw the desire Abimelech had to handle it in a proper way (as much as Abimelech knew how). Abimelech not only had a heart that God could see, but he also had a heart God could speak to.

v. 5 in the integrity of my heart and innocency of my hands have I done this.

v. 6 And God said unto him in a dream, Yea, I know that thou didst this in the integrity of thy heart; for I also withheld thee from sinning against me: therefore suffered I thee not to touch her.

You are right. God does know your heart, its content, and its intent. Have you ever thought, "I wish God would stop me?" Like Abimelech,

God will present you with a way out, but you have to take it.

Why Can't I Overcome?

Why can't I just live holy? It's complicated. Let's take a look at how complicated it is.

There are four entities in this life you will have to contend with in your walk with God. They are God, yourself, your flesh, and the enemy. God is on our side, but the remaining items on this list are not, including yourself. Why have I included yourself? Because although the enemy may have used people to hurt you in the past, it's what you tell yourself about what happened that will continue to harm you long term. The things a person did to you ended at a point in time. The story you tell yourself about the situation is on repeat. So a part of what trips you up is yourself. Your flesh will also hinder you. You know your flesh. It wants five more minutes of sleep in the morning. It wants ice cream at midnight. It wants to steal a parking spot someone else was waiting for. It doesn't want to yield the right-of-way in traffic. In your flesh dwells no good thing (Rom. 7:8). And lastly, you have an adversary-the enemy (I Pet. 5:8). The enemy, a named force of evil (the word Satan means adversary) that is to be resisted (Jam. 4:7), is working to tempt you to lose what God has given you through disobeying God. It takes the power of the Holy Spirit and the armor of God (Eph. 6:10-17) to overcome him.

We Love Our Lives

God requires us to be holy (I Pet. 1:14-16). We are his people. How we steward our frame is a reflection of the God we serve (I Thes. 4:3-5). God has empowered and given us all things that pertain to life and godliness (2 Pet. 1:3). The problem is we don't trust him. We cannot hope to be empowered apart from our trust in him. We will only obey God to the degree we trust him. What will help us trust God? We have to change our perception of him, basing it on what he's provided.

And they overcame him because of the blood of the Lamb and because of the word of their testimony, and they did not love their life even when faced with death.

Revelation 12:11 (NASB)

We cannot overcome because we love our lives too much. Our lives are still OURS! Our lives are not totally God's and we exert minimal effort to make them so. We are gods unto ourselves driving our will, attempting to forge our destinies and we "hire" God as a contractor for short-term projects. In God's design, he calls us unto himself, sets us apart for his use, and empowers us to have a role in his story of love toward humanity. That could happen except we want to be in control. So, we have just enough God in our lives for provision, but not enough for submission and certainly not for commission. We don't want anything that might inconvenience us. The advances and prosperity the church experienced in this age have given way to a self-centered excess, lethargy, and apathy. Most of us are overshadowed by a prayer life that covers the short radius of our desires. Many singles are praying for the salvation of those who catch our eye, but truly have no deep heavenly concern about the soul of the one desired.

The early church was called by God to lay down their lives for their faith and we must too. We must lay down our way of doing things and pick up a kingdom mindset. We need the understanding that we are living for God. He is not living for us.

What Jesus Did for You

Do you not know that your bodies are members of Christ?

... You are not your own

For you have been bought with a price...

I Corinthians 6:15, 19(b), 20(a) (NASB)

There are many stories of native people that were cheated out of their land. In instances where the disenfranchised received an exchange, they were underpaid considering what was traded. Imagine someone comes along and makes a trade with the new owners to overpay for the land, five times, ten times, or a hundred times more than the land was worth and then hands the deed back over to the natives. That is redemption; to buy something back. Jesus didn't just pay what was owed for our unrighteousness. His sacrifice was an overpayment. A pure, eternal life exchanged for a mortal, sin-infested one. That's what makes it a once and for all payment. The payment includes your body and your soul. We will look more closely at this in chapter 5.

Let's go back to our land example. Let's say the natives have their deed back in hand that it cost over a hundred times to get back. The natives get on drugs and sell this deed for $10 and some drugs. This is what happens when you sell yourself short.

What We Have in Christ

We struggle with the word "obey." We find it condescending to be told to "submit." In past centuries, religion has been used to oppress people. Jesus came to set people free (Luke 4:18-21). We have liberty in Christ (Gal. 5:1). We have the freedom and empowerment to obey God because of the sacrifice of Jesus. His shed blood gives us the power to keep God's Word in our daily lives. He is our advocate and restorer when we don't obey (I John 2:1-2). Through Christ, we have the ministry (service and benefit) of reconciliation with God (2 Cor. 5:18-19).

THINK ON THESE THINGS

Who is driving your life? A simple but hard question. If God is driving it, he sets the direction. He sets the course and the destination. If you are driving it, you set the direction. You set the course. We are living epistles (Bibles) read of men (2 Cor. 3:2). As William J. Toms once said, "Be careful how you live; you may be the only Bible some people ever read."[6] Consider the following:

- What does your life say about your relationship with God?

- What have you made greater than God?

- What does "God knows my heart" mean to you?

- Do you struggle with words like "obey" and "submit" in relation to God? If so, Why?

CHAPTER 4 – ABOUT THEM

The Order of Things

There's nothing wrong with making an interest known, but in several instances in the Scriptures, I see a pattern, including first mention. God introduced the first couple to each other. God prepared a woman and introduced her to the man. When I look at Eve, Rebekah, Ruth, Abigail and Esther, God prepared these women then presented them. The women had to meet qualifications of character. God-prepared men such as Adam, Joseph, Job, Boaz and David among others, received opportunities to develop their leadership abilities under God's hand. The introduction is between two prepared people. I am not saying the internet can't introduce you. I am saying, however the introduction comes about, be prepared and qualified.

The Hunt

Men are hunters! I've heard this before. I did not see that in Scripture though. Then God showed me the story of Rebekah and Isaac in Genesis 26.

And Isaac dwelt in Gerar: And the men of the place asked him of his wife; and he said, She is my sister: for he feared to say, She is my wife; lest, said he, the men of the place should kill me for Rebekah; because she was fair to look upon. And it came to pass, when he had been there a long time, that Abimelech king of the Philistines looked out at a window, and saw, and, behold, Isaac was sporting with Rebekah his wife. And Abimelech called Isaac, and said, Behold, of a surety she is thy wife: and how saidst thou, She is my sister? And Isaac said unto him, Because I said, Lest I die for her. And Abimelech said, What is this thou hast done unto us? One of the people might lightly have lien with thy wife, and thou shouldest have brought guiltiness upon us. And Abimelech charged all his people, saying, He that toucheth this man or his wife shall surely be put to death.

Genesis 26:6 – 11 (KJV)

Abimelech had déjà vu. Abraham, Isaac's father, told this lie earlier. Now the second generation is telling this story. Most of the commentaries emphatically point out the sin of lying. No dispute here, but here's what I want you to focus on.

v. 8 …Abimelech king of the Philistines looked out at a window, and saw, and, behold, Isaac was sporting with Rebekah, his wife.

Isaac was sporting with his wife. What is "sporting?" I'm going to show several translations to give you a picture:

The NASB, NIV, NLT versions say, "…Abimelech…saw Isaac _caressing_ his wife."

The Douay-Rheims Bible and Young's Literal Translations say, "…Abimelech…saw Isaac _playing_ with his wife."[7]

The Darby Bible says, "…Abimelech…saw Isaac _dallying_ (to act playfully, especially in an amorous or flirtatious way)[8] with his wife."[9]

Pulpit Commentary refers to sporting as, "Caressing and using playful liberties with her; which showed she was not a sister, but a wife."[10]

So now you have some sense of what the king saw. Here's the deal Reader, Isaac got busted because he was routinely affectionate with his wife. Essentially, Isaac developed a habit of affection with his wife that was so intense and so frequent, and she was so fine, he forgot about that lie he told. You see, if Isaac only "sported" once a month, or to cover up something that went wrong, or only on an anniversary; he wouldn't have gotten caught in his lie. But because he was still busy chasing what he already caught, he got busted!

Look at the lesson here. Isaac married someone that would inspire the chase to continue! In our fallen world, there is only an initial pursuit. But in the kingdom, this playful affection is standard, not optional equipment. Wouldn't it be beautiful to be loved by someone who stays interested in you? Look at God's standard. How far are we from this? There is such a great distance between where we are and God's dreams for us. We need the mindset of Christ to help us close the gap!

Coming Together

God has an expectation of how we will treat each other. He has given us instructions for dealing with people. Love is not easily provoked (I Cor. 6:5). Be kind to one another; forgive one another (Eph. 4:32). Let your "yes" be "yes" and your "no" be "no" (Matt. 5:37).

I had a moment of insight about how we need to treat each other as I was coming on to the highway. As the oncoming lane was merging into the existing lane that already had traffic in it, I realized the two lanes where becoming ONE. There was an interweaving logic to the two lanes merging. Someone would have to pull forward, and someone would have to give way (or as we say in America, "yield").

Christian people want to get married so they can have sex, but run into a myriad of childhood wounds, unresolved family issues, poor communication and inept problem-solving skills that leave the two spouses at each other's throats. The two individual people got married for what they could get from the other person and took no thought as to what they bring to the marriage and what they could give. We are self-centered fallen creatures. Before you get totally offended, let me prove it.

Rob Hill, Sr. from his book, <u>For Single People Who Still Understand the Value of Relationships</u> notes, "The most undervalued part of love is the unconditional part. It's the part of love that allows you to have an orange, your partner to have an apple, but you both agree that it's fruit. Unconditional love is the part of love that understands differences."[11]

We say, "I want someone who loves me unconditionally." However, we show up with defenses and do not present the real self, including the broken, hurting, angry self. We keep this "self" locked up in the basement or attic. We pay the electricity bill and send food to that part of the house, hoping the person we are involved with never meets that self. That is the self that needs love the most. We dishonor that part of ourselves. We do not bring it out into the open. We believe if we reveal that broken, hurting part of ourselves that we will be rejected; left alone. But *we* have rejected it, by not bringing it out. We have abandoned this part of ourselves by giving that pain the misuse of sex, romance, and daydreams instead of bringing it to God to heal. In God-given relationship, he is calling you to a place of peace; rest for your soul (Matt. 11:29).

Special Delivery – A Person

God is sending us a person. Think of something you ordered online – a book or two. The package arrives. The box has brown wrapping paper, packing material or something inside to brace the contents from moving around. It has the items you ordered and a bill. But dealing with a person is not as simple. Even if the exterior matches what you're looking for, you may receive some items on the inside you don't want.

I was searching for a new comforter to cover the bed. I found a good deal at a local store. I hadn't planned to use it yet, but took it out of the package to put it in a space saver bag to store it. I was shocked to find there was no comforter. The sheets that belong to the set were wrapped around two old, stained pillows. I promptly took the whole package back for a refund the same day.

Please be advised dear Reader, God is sending you a person who is that new gift you want, with old pillows inside of it. Each person carries within themselves old wounds and patterns. Some people are willing to address these issues; some are not. Worse, some think they have addressed it, but have merely put a new face on old issues.

We want the benefits of marriage – the validation of worth and attractiveness from a spouse, companionship, so we don't feel alone, children to glean adoration from, and the chemistry of physical intimacy. Does this sound like what you're expecting from marriage? What are you giving in return?

Address Your Wounds

We all want to present our best selves, but the truth is, you have wounds too. You must take responsibility for your wounds. If you get involved with a person because they built up your self-esteem, what happens when they stop? Where was the crack in your esteem? You may have had a hole in your heart, kept open by the messages you tell yourself – "I'm ugly;" "no one wants me," "why does this keep happening to me?" etc. As people pour support and esteem into you, it leaks out. They end up drained and move on. When they leave, they reinforce the negative song you've been singing to yourself. You hope the next relationship will be different. But *you* haven't changed so why would the outcome be different?

How can real intimacy be developed with a person in this condition? The perception of the wounded person is "people leave me." The truth is the environment to sustain a relationship was never created. This person is divided between the everyday person and the hidden wounded person. Until that is reconciled, you cannot have true "togetherness" with another person because you are divided within yourself.

If you are a deeply wounded person, you know how to spot a person who can help you heal. This is the person who confronts you. This is the person you push away.

Think about the scenario of the old wound from a dating perspective. What if sex was introduced into the relationship as the answer for validation, worth, esteem, and companionship? You would have that same emptiness, but you would be chemically bonded. So there would be withdrawal and depression in addition to the negative song being reinforced.

We don't take the time to get to know a person. We are dating for our purposes alone. We will compromise our belief system to get these items we are missing. But remember, God's provision does not require you to break God's Word. He can fulfill all things intended by godly relationship if we are truly using his playbook. The person we encounter belongs to God as his or her Creator. They are a creation of his and were not made for our purposes or desires, but his.

In the Beginning

I've heard it said that God used a rib from the man to fashion woman, so that the woman would be by his side. After some thought, I wanted to look more closely at the function of a rib. It dawned on me that the function of a rib is to protect the heart and the lungs. The first seven ribs are called "true ribs."[12] They are rooted in the spine and reach around the side connecting to the breastbone covering the heart. The rib is a support. The rib is a covering. While the array of ribs is called a cage, ribs are a protective framework that embraces the heart and lungs and holds them secure. Ladies, can you be trusted with his heart and trusted to create that space to breathe? Gentlemen, did you know a woman was to be able to handle essential vulnerable parts and protect them? She has influence and must steward that influence in a godly way.

The ribs partner with the spine, creating a 360-degree protection for the heart and lungs. They are rooted in the spine giving them stability for support, yet they have enough flexibility to move during inhalation and exhalation. The ribs are strong enough to protect, flexible enough to let you breathe. The true ribs support your back so you can stand, come around your side so you can lean, cover your heart so you can be transparent and are flexible enough so you can breathe.

All the ribs can do is maintain their position. If a rib is cracked, it must be mended. If not, it can puncture essentials, it was created to protect. The ribs don't have a defense, but the body will do everything it can to protect that cage. The brain will tell the feet to move away from trouble. The hands will defend the cage because if anything happens to it, the whole body will go down.

Before Eve, Adam received training. He learned how to administrate. He learned how to nurture. He learned how to appropriately determine the purpose of a thing and name it accordingly (Gen. 2:15, 19 -20).

We know that Adam called his rib "woman" (Gen. 2:21-23). From Genesis 3 we also know the devil came in the form of a serpent and deceived the woman. She ate the fruit as Adam stood there silent. Next, she influenced her husband to eat also. This initial disobedience of humanity toward God is known as "The Fall." They sewed aprons out of fig leaves once they realized they were naked. They heard God coming and hid. Adam could have protected Eve, but instead blamed her and God. The woman blamed the serpent. Eating the fruit of the tree of knowledge of good and evil caused death to be released into the earth. God sends an angel to expel Adam and the woman from the garden to prevent them from eating from the tree of life and end up living an eternal death. The couple emerged from this heaven on earth into a wilderness where they had toil in work, the ground was hard, and there would be hardship in pregnancy. They lost their paradise. After all these things, Adam turns to the woman in faith and calls her Eve (Gen. 3:20). This deceived woman and this silent man, who gave occasion for death to reign, are at the end of the worst day of their lives. Adam looks at her and calls her Eve because she was the mother of all living (Gen. 3:20). What a statement! Adam could have named her based on what they lost. He stopped blaming his wife and God and names her based on the hope of their future.

Adam naming his wife Eve (mother of all living), is a point of forgiveness and reconciliation. After Adam makes this statement, then God covers them both. We want God's covering. You have to stay reconciled to get that. They were able to see the worst in each other and forgive each other. Remember, there are no perfect people, but two imperfect people can be perfect for each other. Stand ready to forgive knowing we all stumble in many ways (Jam. 3:2).

THINK ON THESE THINGS

God's paradigm is two prepared adults meeting and supporting each other. His model is being interdependent and staying connected in relationship; as close as the rib, heart, and lungs. Adam and Eve had an intimacy that was free of selfishness before The Fall. Their closeness after this point becomes impaired. Once sin enters, they started hiding, blaming each other and living in fear.

Today, we live in fear of the love we long for. We are still in hiding. The hidden wounded person inside of us gets in the way. We must reconcile ourselves. We must stop showing up as the photograph that comes with a picture frame and show up as our real selves. The people we are meeting deserve that. You can only regard people out of the love you have for yourself. You can't give what you don't have. You cannot "fix" yourself with another person. You have to bring the real you to God, reveal these pain points to him and let him heal you. Only then can you begin to truly benefit as a partner in a relationship. Consider the following:

- Who are you blaming for choices you made?

- What can someone add to your life in a romantic relationship? What can you add to them?

- Why are you hiding your broken self rather than healing it?

- Adam gave Eve a name based on their future. Do you think of yourself based on what you lost or your future?

CHAPTER 5 - ABOUT YOUR BODY

Flee immorality. Every other sin that a man commits is outside the body, but the immoral man sins against his own body. Or do you not know that your body is a temple of the Holy Spirit who is in you, whom you have from God, and that you are not your own? For you have been bought with a price: therefore glorify God in your body.

I Corinthians 6:18 – 20 (NASB)

Temple v. Tool

The body is the temple of the Holy Spirit; the Spirit of God. In sexual immorality, the vehicle (the tool) for sin is the body, just like cigarettes is the tool for one who smokes. This is the sin against your body.

The Apostle Paul draws this contrast between the body as the instrument (the tool) of sin and the body as the temple of the Holy Spirit. Solomon's temple was a beautifully arrayed, sacred space made of cedar and overlaid with gold (I Kings 6). There were qualifications and protocols the priest had to meet for access and service.

The temple represents the presence of God. It represents a place in the earth where God met with his people. Communication took place between God and the people via sacrifice, worship, and prayer. When offerings and sacrifices were made, the smoke would rise high and could be seen in the distance.

Today, the Holy Spirit resides in our human temples; in these bodies. We present these bodies as living sacrifices, holy and acceptable to God (Rom. 12:1). It is not only the body we are presenting. It is our total selves. We withhold nothing from our Redeemer.

Bought with a Price

Do we really understand what we got into by accepting the Lordship of Christ? We are not our own. We were bought with a price (I Cor. 6:20). But what does that mean?

Let's say you're going out of town, and you leave your car with me. While you're gone, I sell it. You get back in town. Sure, you're mad. Then you calm down and ask me how much money I got for it. I say, "$8,000." You say, "OK, where's the money?" I say, "I spent it." What's wrong with this picture? I can offer or sell my car, but I can't offer yours because it doesn't belong to me. And your body doesn't belong to you.

The purity of a believer cannot be traded and is not for sale because our purity has already been purchased at the cost of an infinite life. Christ's death on the cross was the price that was paid. We can't share our bodies because they are not our own. We were bought with a price.

From his book, <u>Sex, Food, and God</u>, Dr. David Eckman writes, "Paul has already told us that God was for the body; that God's love for the body extended beyond the grave because the body will be raised in the resurrection. This body also was joined to Christ. Surely we have a spiritual union with God, but also, a physical union exists between Christ and our bodies. The body was important to God because it is the physical representations of who he is. As persons, we were made to be physical representations of the divine. That representation will go on into eternity itself."[13] So in this life and in the life to come, the body will represent the Lord.

THINK ON THESE THINGS

-Who does your body belong to, you or God?

-In what ways can your stewardship improve in this area?

CHAPTER 6 - ABOUT TEMPTATION

A Seduction

A seduction is like a haunting,
A haze of fog a blinding high
A magnet's pursuit of metal
Longing for contact.
A snowflake looking
To land on your face,
Longing to melt at your touch.
You are hoping
For someone to grab
Your hand.
You aren't expecting
Them to grab your
Attention.
You're hoping
They know
How to keep it.
What else
Do they know
How to keep?
Your thoughts
Overflow with
Possibilities
Spilling into sleep
Blurring fantasy and realities.
Heart pumping,
Mind racing
One look
Spoke to me.

The fire rising beneath my skin
Caresses all oxygen from me.
I lose my head.
I can't breathe.

Your whispers envelop me.
Every ounce of intensity
Says, This moment is
Present for me.

In the future
I will see,
Honey coated emptiness
Lying at my feet.

Every predator
Needs a prey.
I'm falling
Pray for me.

-D Horne 1.26.15

Fighting Temptation

When you're playing with fire, you're going to get burned. First, let's talk about how abundant the choice to do wrong is. In Genesis 4, Cain and Abel were offering sacrifices to the Lord. Cain is a farmer, and Abel is a rancher. Cain offers vegetation (plants). Abel offers meat. Both are first fruits. But Abel's was the best of his first fruits. So God found Abel's offering acceptable, but rejected Cain's. Instead of asking God why his offering was rejected, Cain sulked (pouted). God's response to Cain is in verses 6 and 7.

> 6-7 God spoke to Cain: "Why this tantrum? Why the sulking? If you do well, won't you be accepted? And if you don't do well, sin is lying in wait for you, ready to pounce; it's out to get you, you've got to master it" (MSG).

If you knew you were going to get pounced on, wouldn't you try to defend yourself? The Bible says to step beyond defending yourself against sin and gain mastery over it. The fight is coming to you, whether you want it or not. You will either get bullied or fight back. There are Christians that believe the state of being married will keep them from being attracted to anyone else. Those folks aren't close to being ready to deal with temptation. First, realize there WILL BE temptation!

27

WWLD

Most of us have seen the acronym WWJD, "What Would Jesus Do?" When we go to apply this thought to our situation we think, "I'm not Jesus!" So let me give you a different acronym, WWLD, "What Would Love Do?" We are tempted by things we want. At that moment, it's hard to think of God's will for our lives. We make desperate choices, selfish choices because we are afraid to go unsatisfied if we don't. This is why we look a little too long at someone else when we already have a commitment. This is why we settle for an ill-fitted dating situation rather than remain available. Lust is what fear would do. God has not given us a spirit of fear, but of power and of love and of a sound mind (2 Tim. 1:7).

Why Do We Allow Seduction to Take Place?

It is a combination of desire and attention, wafting around us like incense. A spark begins to smolder. Flames ignite and the blaze roars. You are desired; wanted. Someone wants you bad enough to put on quite a show to get you. And what wants you is telling you it needs you. YOU are what it needs.

Self-esteem is self-value. Attention and being desired is value another places upon you. This is how someone with good esteem can still end up in bed. You can't pay attention to yourself. Someone has to give you attention. Being desired involves a form of affirmation, but the intent and motives of the source can be questionable.

Manipulation is an erosion (wearing away) of the will over time. On the front end, you are being lured (baited) with being wanted. Beneath, your desire to obey God is being worn away. If the person keeps exposing themselves to this influence, over time they will topple (fall).

In a manipulation, we are the center of one's intensity and focus. And they have no problem constantly telling us about it. The praise, admiration, and adulation envelops us. Before this, you may have felt tired, bored or just taken for granted. Now you feel motivated to earn more praise. You feel alive.

The enemy wants you. God does too, but what are they going to do with you once they have you. What is the end goal for both? John 10:10 says, "The thief comes to, kill, steal and destroy, but I came to give you life."

Just as caffeine is a poor substitute for sleep, lust is a poor substitute for love. You begin stepping away from your personhood into a persona. You can get lost in the image you're making. The only way to continue this game you're playing is to hide your heart. You can hide it so well it can become hidden from you. Look out from where you are in relation to your dreams. If you are playing these interludes and intrigues, you are a long way from being a husband and father or a wife and mother. You are an icon in your mirage, but you are a long way from where your deepest desires are. You are a long way from home, and you are not on a road that will take you there.

What's the cost of this illusion? You lose sight of your dreams. You lose sight of yourself. You lose awareness that not everyone plays games. So when you encounter a qualified candidate you're not ready.

Speaking to The Married and Yet to Be Married

When Wanting Goes Wanting

Most of the time, people marry someone they have a desire for. So what happens? Are the cares of this world choking love out? More likely this is what happens:

In the process of being married the veneer of our best dating behavior wears off. You end up seeing behaviors and a lack of consideration that you DON'T want in the person you wanted. As a result, your desire for them fades. This is why the biggest fuel for maintaining passion is honesty because then what you want is the person and not their presentation. But people are still standing in fig leaves, hiding who they are.

While we're here, let's talk about unfaithfulness. Before you can be full of "un-faith," you have to lose faith in what you have. As faith drains out, you begin to fill up on disconnection and apathy. Just beyond apathy is a sense of entitlement. "I deserve to have…" "I deserve to be happy." The "I deserve" has to show up to justify the actions that follow it. At the time you notice apathy, fight it with thankfulness. Thankfulness can re-fuel your faith and stop the leak before it becomes a flood.

Fear or Faith

Many Christians are what I call, "door crack" Christians. Every time the doors of the church open, they are there. A lot of these folks are afraid they will revert to their old ways if they are not at church 24 hours a day 7 days a week. That's fine for newer believers who are still on the "milk" of the Word, but God did not call us to live in fear of falling. He can keep us from falling (Jude 1:24). According to I John 4:4, you have Jesus on the inside of you, who is greater than any advertisement, text, phone call, or opportunity you will receive for temptation.

Instead of walking in fear, walk in wisdom. The Bible tells us what to do with lust. Flee (run from/turn down the opportunity). Don't stand there and "pray about it!"

Flee fornication

I Corinthians 6:18 (KVJ)

Submit yourselves therefore to God. Resist the devil and he will flee from you.

James 4:7 (KVJ)

No temptation has overtaken you except what is common to mankind. And God is faithful; he will not let you be tempted beyond what you can bear. But when you are tempted, he will also provide a way out so that you can endure it.

I Corinthians 10:13 (NIV)

As far as living godly, there's a God part and a "you" part. God can provide the way of escape, but you have to take it.

Humility - An Exchange

> Come to me, all of you who are weary and carry heavy burdens, and I will give you rest. Take my yoke upon you. Let me teach you because I am humble and gentle at heart, and you will find rest for your souls. For my yoke is easy to bear, and the burden I give you is light.
>
> Matthew 11:28-30 (NLT)

In exchange for the weariness of our burdens, Jesus offers rest. To get this rest, we must take up his yoke. A yoke is a framework that allows two entities to move together as one. This also causes the load of one to be distributed among the framework. In farm culture, two animals are teamed together. To accept Christ's yoke, we have to give up control. In Risking Intimacy, author Nancy Groom says of her marriage, "We had become experts at managing our lives and defending our own behavior, and it felt altogether foreign to rest in God instead of in our resources."[14] We have to let God be God. We must surrender to him.

Surrender

Two things intersect for surrender to occur. One, you have to be tired of where you are. Two, you have to willing to believe God's way of doing things is better than your way of handling it. Sometimes our greatest temptation is to keep doing the same thing the same way.

THINK ON THESE THINGS

Temptation involves choice. I used to think the problem with the Garden of Eden was the tree of the knowledge of good and evil. The occupants would have been better off without that tree. But without that tree, there would be no choice. We have temptation, such that is common to man, the lust of the eyes, the lust of the flesh and the pride of life (I Cor. 10:13; I John 2:16). With all of those options, God still wants us to put him first, as our choice, not a default. This is why we have free will. Consider the following:

-What will it cost you to choose temptation?

-What is the difference between God's desire for you and what is being offered?

-What will you do differently the next time temptation comes knocking?

CHAPTER 7 – ABOUT HONOR

The Honor Principle

> For this is the will of God, your sanctification; that is, that you abstain from sexual immorality; that each of you know how to possess his own vessel in sanctification and honor, not in lustful passion, like the Gentiles who do not know God.

> I Thessalonians 4:3 – 5 (NASB)

This is the passage that started the ball rolling for me. I began thinking there must be a way to possess my vessel and that doing so would reflect my knowing God. Upon reviewing this passage, the word 'honor' stood out to me. Here, not having sex is tied to honor. There is another passage where the word honor is mentioned with having sex, Hebrews 13:4.

> Let marriage be held in honor (esteemed worthy, precious, of great price, and especially dear) in all things. And thus let the marriage bed be undefiled (kept undishonored); for God will judge and punish the unchaste [all guilty of sexual vice] and adulterous.

> Hebrews 13:4 (AMP)

So here is the parallel, as a single, God's will for us is to possess our vessel in honor by sanctification, setting our body aside for the Lord and abstaining from sex. In marriage, God's will for the covenanted couple is to honor their union. Honor in marriage includes sex. Your body is set aside for your spouse.

Many hang-ups concerning sex from the Christian perspective are based on teaching sex as being "nasty" or "unclean." This approach may have taken place to discourage promiscuity, but sex being "nasty" in and of itself is clearly not scriptural. Sex is clean, and we have to keep our view of it as precious and honorable.

In the Old Testament, the word honor comes from the verb "ka-bad" meaning "heavy, weighty, or burdensome."[15] There are several ways this can be looked at, "achieving honor, growing stronger, laid burdens, your glory, etc."[16] The heaviness is perceptible. There is a result that reaches a public view. For the Hebrews passage in Greek, the word is *Timios,* which means honored among others (publicly respected or having an honorable reputation).[17]

Consider an Olympic athlete. The audience that watches the Olympic event wasn't there for the athlete's training. There was something that went on in private (years of training and practice), the fruit of which displays itself in a way that results in a win, for which they are honored in public.

In singleness, we sanctify ourselves, we set ourselves apart, just as the athlete sets themselves apart to train. Celibacy is a discipline unto God. You will need to know this discipline. According to I Thessalonians 4, you possess your vessel rather than your vessel possessing you. Mastering that will be important, not only as a reflection of your relationship with God and your value and worth as a single, but it is critical for those who aspire to marry. Paul makes a clear statement in I Corinthians 6, when you are single, your body is for the Lord (v. 18 -20). In I Corinthians 7, Paul speaks to the married and says your body is not your own, but belongs to your mate and your mate's body belongs to you. For the single, abstaining from sex is a point of honor. For the married, their sexual fellowship is to be kept pure and their union held in high regard.

So the picture of honor is a lesser known (private) diligence resulting in public praise. Honor is NOT done in secret. There is usually an honor-er and an honor-ee. Honor involves worth. You are considered worthy to be honored; priceless, precious. Someone worthy of honor can be considered excellent or supreme, in its class; or in a class of its own.

In the context of Hebrews 13:4, sex is connected to the marriage's reputation. As believers, we are known by the way we love one another (John 13:35). In the context of marriage, physical intimacy of the marital union is a part of that love. Sex is already pure because it has been set apart by God for marriage. It is up to the individual to maintain the purity God gave it or make it impure.

Honor is a form of validation. You are making known what this person means to you. To receive an honor can elicit feelings of humility. To be honored, you have to receive. You are not in control. Can you allow yourself to be honored?

The "weight" of honor is consistent treatment in private, in public and in intimacy. What makes the union honorable is the value of the relationship remains high in every setting. This value comes across in how we speak to each other; the way we fight; the way we make up; the way the partners consider the feelings of their mate. Honor is the intersection of love and respect.

Love, particularly in the sexual area, can become intermittent or shallow as a reaction to the partner's behavior. So then sex simply becomes an act. The heart is wearing a condom. Respect can be the same way. Respect becomes intermittent based on a reaction to the partner's behavior. So the spouse respects the role of spouse but not the person anymore. Regard is how I feel about you. Respect is about how I treat you. So the respect becomes intermittent when you disappoint me. Honor takes place when we keep the "weight" of our regard high in the face of disappointment. Now, I'm not saying to hold a person of seriously cracked character and lack of commitment in high regard. Honor is earned. Only keep in mind, a lot of times intimacy dies a death of 1,000 cuts and our faith in the relationship pours out of each cut.

Love seeks to keep high regard and from that high regard, the basis of respect is derived. So it behooves us to select people of integrity. Select someone we want to forgive; someone we want to continue loving. Select people who inspire us to hold them in high regard.

Now that we have visited honor, love, and respect, Paul has connected these things to the marriage bed. What needs to take place for a mate to feel honored in bed? To be honored is to be appreciated and celebrated. There is no selfishness in honoring someone.

THINK ON THESE THINGS

Sex has been an area of embarrassment for many Christians because we have not handled it well; it has handled us. God looks for us to carry ourselves in a way that retains our honor. Here's a depiction of Mordecai being honored from the book of Esther.

> For the man the king delights to honor, have them bring a royal robe the king has worn and a horse the king has ridden, one with a royal crest placed on its head. Then let the robe and horse be entrusted to one of the king's most noble princes. Let them robe the man the king delights to honor, and lead him on the horse through the city streets, proclaiming before him, 'This is what is done for the man the king delights to honor!

> Esther 6:7-9 (NIV)

Consider the following:

-You are looking for someone who turns you on. Does that person know how to honor you?

- God wants you to be honored for your virtue. What would that look like for you as a single person? As a married person?

-What would make you feel honored?

CHAPTER 8 – ABOUT SEX

Chemistry - You Complete Me

Many people will tell you being complete on your own is necessary for a healthy relationship. While that is true, permit me to clarify this sense of "completion" as an experience. Many singles are very busy people. We still desire a romantic relationship, but the space we have in our hearts for another, we fill with ambition, duty or busyness. Since we cannot experience the fulfillment, we experience a distraction from a lack of fulfillment. Imagine you are at a restaurant and placed an order with your server. While you are waiting for your meal, you may enjoy a beverage and bread or an appetizer, but that is not the main course. The satisfaction of the order comes from completion of your desired outcome.

Part of what makes sex an ethereal, satisfying experience are chemicals in the brain. Oxytocin is a brain chemical that produces feelings of trust and attachment. Men get a blast of it when they kiss; women feel a rush when they hold a lover's hand.[18]

Biological anthropologist Dr. Helen Fisher has studied relationships for nearly thirty years. She offers three key components of love, involving different, but connected brain systems:[19]

Lust — driven by sex hormones testosterone (androgen) and estrogen, the craving for sexual gratification

Attraction — driven by high dopamine and norepinephrine levels and low serotonin, romantic or passionate love, characterized by euphoria when things are going well, terrible mood swings when they're not, focused attention, obsessive thinking, and intense craving for the individual

Attachment — driven by the hormones oxytocin and vasopressin, the sense of calm, peace, and stability one feels with a long-term partner

We are talking about attraction here. As you spend more time with your love interest, the very thought of them, every moment with them floods your brain with these chemicals and gives a sense of euphoria. This feeling of fulfillment is temporary, but it can be termed "completeness" by the person experiencing it. The medical definition of euphoria is "a feeling of well-being or elation; *especially:* one that is groundless, disproportionate to its cause, or inappropriate to one's life situation."[20]

Wrapped in the arms of the one you love, you will experience feelings of calm, serenity, feeling full or utter satisfaction. The experience will tell you no different. You may feel a connection so deep you swear you can live off it. You'll wonder if you've ever hugged, kissed or touched a person before because you are experiencing something so sublime, so unparalleled.

Many seek to spiritualize this experience as a sign that this is "the one." Others go too far, too fast, end up in bed with the object of their desire and can't stop obsessing over them. In some religious circles, this is referred to as "soul ties." Not that there isn't a spiritual force at work. Licentiousness means lacking moral restraint, especially in sexual conduct.[21] If your desires are outweighing self-control, there is a spiritual issue because part of the work of the Holy Spirit is to produce self-control in the life of the believer (Gal. 5:23). Or it could be the beginning of a healthy relationship, but your mind is flooded with romance and you need balance to get back on track. In either case, there is a "you" part and a God part. A brain that is flooded can be unflooded, just as we busied ourselves before and focused on something else.

The reason we keep returning to thoughts of connection, fulfillment and being the focus of someone's desire is because we want to experience being loved. We want to live in love. That desire to be loved is pure. The important point is how we go about fulfilling it. I believe the euphoria, temporary though it may be, is an intended gift we were meant to experience in love. Romance has sizzle, but it is up to you to make sure the eggs in the pan are pure, fresh and not spoiled because even a rotten egg can be fried!

Soul Ties

I have also encountered Christians praying prayers to break soul ties, renouncing their lovers by name in prayers and casting out spirits of lust. The late comedian Flip Wilson used to have a comedic line about how "the devil made me do it." With the barrage of beauty, desire and temptation in advertising and the media, our senses are inundated. The spirit behind it seeks to create endless unmet desire. However, how we are tied to people is more layered than that.

Fears Without, A Fight Within

It takes time to develop a habit. So, for a time, the person you were involved with (or the daydream you were involved with), may have become a habit. Then there is what the person said to you during your interaction that stayed in your head. You believed it. In addition, there is what you told yourself about what happened.

So no, I don't think Honey or Pookie has been working ungodly spiritual forces to leave their house and crawl into bed with you. While practitioners do exist, by and large, I believe you're either:

-afraid you can't get anyone else

-still angry at your ex for a particular issue

-trying to re-create an old relationship with a new co-star

-or reheating your memories of your ex to keep you warm and stave off loneliness

So yes, people may still be in your soul (mind, will and emotions). I think we replay scenes in our mind that we experienced. They may have stopped reaching out to you, but you are holding on to them. Are you hanging on to familiar things? Some ways we hang on is through anger, unforgiveness, or fear of being alone. In those cases, we need to accept the right to be free of the anger and ask God to help us to forgive them. We may need to forgive ourselves as well to close the wound. We are not alone. Remember, God will help you to live free and honorably.

What is Purity?

We will only obey God to the degree we trust him. Therefore, the areas of our lives where we are inconsistent to God's Word (disobedient), we do not trust him. If we do not trust God, we do not surrender those things to him, and he is not Lord over it. So the goal of purity is not merely sexual morality, but to give God his rightful place as Lord in our lives. We think of purity as the absence of something. The Lordship of Christ in this area is the presence of something. It is the presence of a statement of faith - faith in God's provision, God's order, God's timing, God's taste, God's overall plan for your life. When you have faith in these things, it will show up in your actions. Purity, in this case, is a result of your faith. You are doing something. You are waiting on God and believing in him. Your demonstration of this belief is your purity. Purity is the presence of something – a trust in God. A lack of purity is a demonstration of our not trusting him.

How We See Sex

We see sex as a right; an entitlement we have promoted to a need. A need so strong we marry for it. However, in taking this approach with it, we give it power over us and in part, we give it the ability to shorten our relationship and minimize the relationship's power.

In the Long Run

I was surprised by how many men like the movie, The Notebook. The film shows a couple from various points in time. We see them as lovers in their late teens. Then in their mid-twenties. We see them in pictures in their 40's and 50's. We see them lastly in their late 70's and 80's. What we want at each of these stages changes. The shopping list you had at 20 will look somewhat different at 50. I bring this up because we say we want someone to grow old with, but we don't shop like it.

The role and frequency of sex changes with age. Over time, general health requires much more maintenance. Some medications designed to stave off one malady can present complications for sexual health, not to mention the mental challenges of aging. In the movie, <u>The Notebook,</u> a husband makes a sacrifice of his personal comforts to live in a medical facility with his spouse. He is still healthy enough for intimacy, but his spouse is suffering from a form of dementia. He has to conduct himself as if he's on a first date with the woman who is his wife of over 40 years and the mother of his children. She's in love with him when she remembers who she is and afraid of him when she doesn't. We want to be loved that much, but we're not willing to go that far or be inconvenienced.

For many people seeking a spouse, sex is a deal breaker. The potential mate either needs to be pure as the driven snow or an exotic dancer that got saved 5 minutes ago. You are packing summer clothes with no expectation of life's winters. You can't pack for marriage like you're packing for a weekend. Marriage is for a lifetime.

Pray It Away?

> God has created us in such a way as to prevent hesitancy and withdrawal from love. He does not want us to give up on the search for intimacy. He desires that we form positive, nurturing relationships with himself and others. God created us with a built-in guarantee that we would not give up on love. Our sexuality is this guarantee. Sexuality is God's insurance that we will continue to be relational individuals. Rather than withdrawing from others, sexuality continues to draw us into others. Thus, our sexuality is a gift from God, one of His ways to ensure that we will seek loving relationships with those different from us.[22]

> -Rick Stedman, <u>Your Single Treasure</u>

I present Stedman's perspective to you, Reader, because I wanted to bring a voice that would speak to the Christian whose response to sexuality is to ask God to take away their sexual drive. As you've seen from the chemistry section, you were created with a sex drive. You can still have a sex drive and live for God, just make God lord over it like all the other parts of your life.

How Sex Reflects God

> Then the Sadducees, who say there is no resurrection, came to him
> with a question. "Teacher," they said, "Moses wrote for us that if a
> man's brother dies and leaves a wife but no children, the man must
> marry the widow and raise up offspring for his brother. Now there
> were seven brothers. The first one married and died without leaving
> any children. The second one married the widow, but he also died,
> leaving no child. It was the same with the third. In fact, none of the
> seven left any children. Last of all, the woman died too. At the
> resurrection whose wife will she be, since the seven were married to
> her?" Jesus replied, "Are you not in error because you do not know
> the Scriptures or the power of God? When the dead rise, they will
> neither marry nor be given in marriage; they will be like the angels in
> heaven."

> Mark 12:18-27 (NIV)

As the Sadducees attempt to debate Jesus about resurrection, Jesus
revealed something about the nature of the life to come. Believers will not
marry or be given in marriage, according to v. 27. We will be like angels in
heaven. Mankind is made a little lower than the angels (Ps. 8:5). Our bodies
are finite and fleshly. Angelic frames are heavenly and infinite. I raise this
issue to tell you there is no sex in heaven or eternity. It's obvious if God's
context for sex is marriage, and Jesus says there will be no marriage in
resurrection, then there will clearly NOT be sex in heaven or eternity. This
is not some sort of punishment. The experience of physical intimacy, sex, is
a reflection of a greater oneness that comes from being in the presence of
God and a fellowship with him in an infinite frame that can handle it. Sex
is a prelude to what is to come. If you can't imagine life without sex, try to
imagine an eternity in an experience with God that is even greater than that!
Intimacy in the next life is so far beyond our comprehension that we need a
whole other body to experience it! Thank God he is giving us bodies that
can handle it!

God is Intimate

Our sexuality reflects a facet of God's image. Author Rick Stedman notes, "(theologian) Karl Barth described sexuality as the "God-like" in us, by this, he did not mean that God was sexually differentiated. Instead, our sexuality displays our ability and inclination to be relating people. We are created with the inborn ability and need to relate to others. We are designed to be in relationship. The image of God in us, according to Genesis 1:27, is our ability to relate and share intimacy. It is, therefore when we love others and allow ourselves to be loved that we most reflect the image of God."[23]

God is intimate. God wrapped himself in flesh (John 1:1; 14). He opened his heart and his body and invited us into himself through the cross. The cross is the fulfillment of a promise of redemption, a demonstration of covenant love toward mankind (Rom. 5:8-11). As we receive him as Savior and Lord, he gives us his innocence. He spreads himself over us, enveloping us in an embrace that splits time into eternity. We become one with him. For we are a fragrance of Christ to God among those who are being saved and among those who are perishing; to the one an aroma from death to death, to the other an aroma from life to life (2 Cor. 2:15 - 16 NIV). We are drawn closer to Christ in surrender to him. Our relationship with Christ gets deeper as we yield to him. We relive this intimacy through prayer and the sacrament of communion.

God is intimate. He is in every touch, every glance, every caress. Author Gary Thomas notes, "He is the architect and creator of sex. Just as the sex drive calls us out of ourselves and into another, God calls us out of our self-centeredness and into himself.[24]

Can I ever escape him (God)? No. He is in everything. Even in a kiss.[25]

- The Count of Monte Cristo (Film)

God is intimate. We bear his image and likeness. Through Christ, we have the opportunity to bear God's intimate nature. And with the guidance of the Holy Spirit, we actively strive towards maturity to be the expression of that nature in the earth.

One facet of a conquest is surrender. There is one so persistent, so powerful; the other has no choice but to yield. God pursues us throughout our lifespan. He patiently persists as we put people and things before him. As we turn toward him, the layers of guilt, unworthiness, disappointment, and regret peel away. He longs to bring us back to a place where we are naked and not ashamed; loved for who we are rather than what we have or what we do. He receives us unto himself and clothes us in righteousness. God is looking for more than two hours once a week with you. He wants intimacy because God is intimate.

He shapes the curves and clefts of our frames. He gives us the kiss of life and makes us living souls. We abide under his shadow. Under his wings we trust, we feel safe and whole. God is intimate.

God is the only lover we never ask what he desires, what he likes. What does he want you to look like? He prefers you to be clothed in righteousness. Your righteousness is from him. Consider it as a necklace, a chain with a pendant that bears his mark. You're wearing it is a sign that you are distinctly his. It swings between you two when you become one. The earth can feel the vibration of your presence because you are filled with him. He explodes from you as a fire that cannot be contained. Your praise moves him as you call out his name. He draws near to you. The heavens sigh, "Lord, you're worthy. Lord, most high." God is intimate.

We are selfish lovers. We don't ask God, how he feels. We don't ask how we can give him pleasure. We're too afraid to ask, but not afraid to take. Our passion is absent. Our backs are turned. We're asleep again. God is awake lying next to us; waiting for us to wake up. Will you even look at him? God is intimate.

This Present Life

When it comes to sex, we perceive God is keeping something from us rather than preparing something for us. Keep in mind God is Love (I John 4:8). He is not merely loving; he is love itself. The Bible's physical expression of love is in the Song of Solomon.

How beautiful are thy feet with shoes, O prince's daughter! The joints of thy thighs are like jewels, the work of the hands of a cunning workman. Thy navel is like a round goblet, which wanteth not liquor: thy belly is like an heap of wheat set about with lilies. Thy two breasts are like two young roes that are twins. Thy neck is as a tower of ivory; thine eyes like the fishpools in Heshbon, by the gate of Bath-rabbim: thy nose is as the tower of Lebanon which looketh toward Damascus. Thine head upon thee is like Carmel, and the hair of thine head like purple; the king is held in the galleries. How fair and how pleasant art thou, O love, for delights! This thy stature is like to a palm tree, and thy breasts to clusters of grapes. I said, I will go up to the palm tree, I will take hold of the boughs thereof: now also thy breasts shall be as clusters of the vine, and the smell of thy nose like apples; and the roof of thy mouth like the best wine for my beloved, that goeth down sweetly, causing the lips of those that are asleep to speak. I am my beloved's, and his desire is toward me.

Song of Solomon 7:1-10 (KJV)

In this text, Solomon is ravishing his bride. In previous chapters, they had a discord and are now reunited. God permitted this glimpse into the early days of a newlyweds' bedroom to be chronicled in Scripture. God created sexual passion and sheltered it in marriage, much like a fire safely and securely raging in a fireplace. This fire brings light and heat in the warm glow of its crackle. Do not believe for one second God wishes to withhold passion from you. He is looking to prepare you for it, much like an oven mitt or a motorcycle helmet. No man can take fire to his bosom and not get burned (Prov. 6:27). Passion is only one facet of love. The provision of our God is abundant and multifaceted.

Impurity (Defilement)

The marriage bed is honorable in all and undefiled (Heb. 13:4). Sex as God designed it is clean. What skews our view of it is the context. The context of sex in marriage is beautiful and honorable. When sex is something we trade for provision or to manipulate people, we have treated something extraordinary as something common. This is defilement. I know you're expecting me to talk about furry handcuffs and paraphernalia here, but I'm going to talk about the most common forms of defilement.

Based on how we treat sex, I don't think we were properly introduced to it. Beyond the scientific introduction, sex becomes known to us by how we acquire it. Sex becomes a sport, a right, an entitlement to be obtained regardless of cost. In short, sex becomes a game of takers. The word "rape" comes from the Latin *rapere*; it means "to seize."[26] Virtue was taken without consent. So to satiate the libido and assuage the conscience, "the game" or seduction is used.

This is not a new practice. The poet Ovid, who lived from 25 – 1 BC, wrote <u>Ars Amatoria (Art of Love),</u> which gives us a window into seduction in ancient Rome. Ovid stipulates, in a businesslike fashion, that promising the moon is a helpful way to a girl's bedroom.[27]

To say someone has "game" usually means they are skillfully charming. That is different from "running game" or "playing games" which means the person is insincere; doing and saying whatever they can to get what they want from you. There are genuine romances, and then there is "game." Game is based on the pursuit of sexual disenfranchisement with consent. It is the erosion of will over time. The game is a manipulation, a seduction that must involve your "yes." It is a means to an end labeled as fun.

So here's what happened. Some women became aware of the game. They learned the rules and figured out they are the ones who have the ball. The game ends when you take your ball and go home. This is a woman with a scarred heart, who has experienced disappointment and has become disillusioned. You show up when she calls. You can leave when she's bored.

Then there's the other end of the spectrum. A woman allows herself to become physically involved, but actually isn't with it. The man and woman eventually marry. The man starts encountering less sex than before the marriage. Why? Resentment. Not to say all women are not willing participants, but in this case, the woman sided against herself to get something she wanted (a husband) more than her integrity (how she really felt) and now the marriage is in place with a crack in its foundation.

She sees what happened as a game and has taken her ball and gone home in the marriage. This is a punitive manipulation. This is defilement. The man ran game to get the woman. The woman used herself to get the man. Now neither are happy with what they have. What do they have? Marriage defiled with selfishness. Un-love and disrespect. The complete opposite of what the Word says. This is dishonor.

When a man pursues, a woman's sexual "no" to turn it into a "yes," every step he makes towards the "yes" is a step further away from her trust. Even if you get what you want and then marry her, she will curl up every night with that distrust instead of you.

The woman, in this case, is also responsible here. She had a weak "no." When you have a weak "no", you cannot have a strong "yes." A weak "no" means you're not committed to yourself. A weak yes means you're not going to follow through on your word to others. Ironically, she doesn't trust this man, but it is also clear she doesn't mean what she says so he shouldn't trust her either. Distrust, un-love, and disrespect.

No Peeking

If someone were to say to you, let's peek into someone's window and watch them get undressed would you do that? Or hide in a closet to watch a couple in their bedroom being intimate, would you do that? Probably not, yet we watch it on television. One of the dangers of romance novels, movies, and television, is the ability to lose sight of the individual's personhood and simply view them as objects. Certainly, this happens with pornography.

In pornography, everything is solved with sex. The personhood is eroded, and the person becomes identified as an activity. The porn star or the stripper is not a person; they are a personification of sex to the observer. They need to keep that illusion to get paid. In the process, you become what you watch, and sex becomes a god because it solves everything it touches in the show. But what is it turning you into? You become an object in your own mind. How can you expect to be loved as a whole person when you are an object in your own mind?

Intimacy infers privacy. So when a married couple invites other people into their intimacy, it becomes something else. Whether it is a real person or images, spouses end up compared to unrealistic images and standards that bring with it challenges to intimacy. Sex in a marriage should be affirming. Comparisons make it difficult to appreciate what you have. Many liaisons started from unthankfulness and a lack of appreciation for what they already have during a moment of discord.

I'll Handle it Myself

By definition, self-pleasuring is self-centered and is counterintuitive to your goal of relationship. The goal of relationship is two becoming one. That cannot be created in isolation. Self-pleasuring can involve fantasy, imagery, gadgetry and objects. In the process of these indulgences, what happens to your view of physical intimacy? As you gain sexual self-awareness arousing yourself, eventually your own hands won't be enough. Desire increases because whatever you feed (more effort and frequency) grows. You will begin to look for other hands; people to do what your hands, your gadget or the website does. Of course, it will be an "even trade." You'll pleasure them in exchange for what you receive. And this is the trap. Over time, you will realize you've begun making objects of people. What you don't see is you've become an object in your own eyes. You started this pursuit of self-pleasure. It's just you. You need to feel comforted. It won't hurt anybody. In the end, you are using others, including yourself. Once you start using yourself, it gives license for others to do the same. You become convenient. You are so far away from the relationship, commitment or family you once desired. We cling on to temporary things while not preparing for something real. Stop playing games with yourself.

Fifty Shades of Marriage

Now, what about those furry handcuffs? What if you're a married couple? Handcuffs? Remember the over-arching goal. Not everything is for everybody. Consider these things as candy. It involves personal preference, and it cannot substitute for a meal. Visit only on terms of mutual consent, but be warned this is an area you can't afford to live in. This moving into your everyday world becomes a problem because things like this tend to escalate. Don't be so busy making your sex life spicy the rest of the marriage chokes. Make sure your finances are spicy, your communication is spicy, your family goals are spicy, and your relationship with God is spicy. Do you get what I'm saying?!

Undisclosed Trauma

Let's make one more stop. Some people say they want to wait until marriage. They are securing the validation of a spouse's love by getting a commitment first. But the commitment is not going to deal with the real issue. They have an undealt with assault in this area. Sexual assault carries with it traumatic memories. The ability to fully experience intimacy or affection is deeply impaired. Your fiancé is flying blind into the turbulence in your soul and will constantly be repelled by you thinking there's something wrong with them.

In this situation, the present is being polluted with the past. Your intimacy is being held hostage. But how do you tell someone you're broken? One of our deepest fears is if someone really knew us, they wouldn't want us. Marriage is a huge affirmation. But concealing a matter like this prevents the opportunity for someone to step into this tender place with you and love you where you are. That would create real intimacy with the right person. Instead of something distant, barely tolerable and strained, you have the opportunity to experience something beautiful becoming one with one who loves you; one torso, one heart, one breath as man and woman were before, collapsing into one sweet repose. The marriage bed is pure and undefiled (Heb. 13:4).

THINK ON THESE THINGS

Good, Better, Best

-It's not *good* that man should be alone. (Gen. 2:18)

-It is *better* to marry than to burn. (I Cor. 7:9)

-It is *best* to learn how to possess your vessel. (I Thes. 4:1-8)

How are you doing with each of these?

CHAPTER 9 – ABOUT LOVE

There is a big difference between God's love and our love. God is love according to I John 4:8. God is love, but he is not sex. Many times sex is the means by which people try to attain love. If you are exchanging sex for love, you are attempting to make a purchase. Love can't be bought. True love is priceless. When God decided to demonstrate his love to mankind, he did it on the cross (Rom. 5:8). Jesus gave an infinite life on your behalf. In this, God says, "I love you plus infinity." You will never out-love God.

Love and Comfort

A relative of mine sent me an e-mail requesting prayer as he was in route to donate a kidney to his friend. He was asking for prayer that the operation would be successful and that the recipient's body would accept the kidney. God answered that prayer. As I read this email, I realized I was looking at a demonstration of what real love looks like. My relative took off time from work and flew out of state to donate the kidney. Love is not convenient and can make you uncomfortable.

When we approach dating and love relationships, we dress for the purpose of arousal, hope the date involves some intrigue and usually skip anything that would require building a friendship. If this person both excites and attracts us, and they give us the opportunity to be physical, we may take it. Over a brief period of time, we may give our physical selves to this person. We open our bodies to people that we would not leave in our homes if we weren't there. We give our bodies to people we would never give our ATM financial access code to. As I thought of these two different scenarios I saw the truth converging. On one hand, true love donates its kidney. On the other, true lust donates other appendages. So let me ask you, Reader, both of these items are on your body, would you give the kidney to the same person you gave the "cookie" (your sexual parts) to?

Your whole body is valued because Christ died for it. In God's design, the person you share your body with should be someone who would give you a kidney, but first you give each other a commitment via marriage covenant. Within society, love is determined by value. People respond to the value you place on yourself. It is rare to find a person who will value you more than you do. But there is one who does, and he is Jesus Christ.

Do You Really Want to Love?

People usually want marriage because it comes with sex, but marriage is a covenant of inconvenience where one has many opportunities to display grace daily because as James 3:2 says we stumble in many ways. Marriage is a ministry of reconciliation. The physical union in marriage is another form of reconciliation whereby a man and woman who originally shared one form are reunited and thereby reconciled. It is ironic that marriage is frequently broken under the description of irreconcilable differences. So then marriage should not be undertaken by people who have trouble forgiving or like holding grudges because they are not prepared to maintain a ministry of reconciliation.

Intimacy

In physical intimacy, we disrobe. You will come to bed bare-bodied, hairy and coarse, short or fat, tall or skinny, scarred, wrinkled, freckled, with all your imperfections. And yet we come to love with our clothes still on. We say we want to be loved for our true selves as we clutch our fig leaves.

It is a very powerful thing to be the object of someone's sole focus; to be desired, pedestalized, fawned over, and all the other things that physical intimacy brings with it. Many times we didn't really love whoever we were intimate with, we loved the attention they paid us as well as the pleasure they gave us. The difference is that when we are in love, we get pleasure from knowing that person and desire them to be our main source of pleasure because there is no pleasure without them. The exclusivity of such love demands commitment.

Vulnerability

There is a difference in being transparent and vulnerability. Transparency is done for accountability and for setting an example. Vulnerability occurs when you reveal an area that needs strengthening to someone who can bring strength. Otherwise, it is an announcement to a predator, a mocker or someone who is indifferent.

Your vulnerability is an access point into your heart. The Bible says to guard your heart with all diligence (Prov. 4:23). Take a tip from your software companies. They don't publicly announce their vulnerabilities. They announce the software patch.

When a software company finds a vulnerability, they announce the vulnerability to an in-house team of software engineers who design protection (a patch for the hole in the software). The engineers sign a Non-Disclosure Agreement. They cannot discuss the matter openly until the patch is released to the public. Do not announce your vulnerability to the public at large. Announce the patch.

When Are You Vulnerable?

I was carrying too many packages because I didn't want to make more than one trip to the car. I realized as I wobbled up to the door, that if something required my immediate attention, I would have to stop, drop everything and address it. I realized I was vulnerable. Do you have a physical blind spot? Are you overcommitted? Are you lonely? Are you tired? Then you are vulnerable. What's your plan for a patch?

Sacrifice

Godly love requires sacrifice. Your living pure is a form of sacrifice. You are presenting your body as a living sacrifice, holy and acceptable unto God (Rom. 12:1). As you preserve the other person by not tempting them, you sacrifice your ego. These things represent your need to put the one you love ahead of your own will and desires. Doing that for God certainly gives you the practice to sacrifice for those you love. Would you want to end up in bed with someone who is only focused on their own self-interests? What kind of lover would they be? God doesn't want that for you either. Love seeks not its own (1 Cor. 13:5).

The Cost

You want to be loved. What price are you willing to pay for it? Ultimately, if you desire to marry, you will pay for that with your independence and your singleness among other things. Quite often you'll hear an "independent woman" say she can't find a man. When she enters a relationship, she continues to assert the "independent woman" song. A relationship requires interdependence. Then there's the person who loves to give gifts but hates receiving. Love also requires a willingness to be served. Many of us fear this because to let someone serve us, takes us out of the driver's seat. We are not in control. One of the lessons love seeks to teach us is how to receive. Remember Peter had a problem letting Jesus wash his feet (John 13:3–9)? The lesson of relationship teaches us interdependence; we can rely on one another's strengths and secure (patch) our vulnerabilities.

There are many people who say the gift of salvation is free. It is to the recipient. But salvation cost Jesus dearly. He had to be wrapped in human flesh, submit to the humiliation of being a baby, wait to grow up, start a ministry, be rejected, betrayed, beaten, falsely accused and openly killed. And it will cost you something to follow Jesus. You have to put down your playbook to pick up his will for your life. Real love will begin to assess the cost of getting involved with you – time, freedom, potential additional dependents, additional finances, social circles, other obligations, etc. in the face of their own dreams. Love is looking to grow old with you. Love endures (1 Cor. 13:7). Love sees a need and meets the need.

How do you know when you're really in love and not just emotion? Love comes not merely in words, but in deeds and truth (I John 3:18). You can tell love about your real self and love won't love you less. You can hear the truth about yourself from love and your love for that person will not diminish.

THINK ON THESE THINGS

God paid a price to maintain his relationship with man. He paid the price of a Son, Jesus. The greatest value God placed on you was himself. Through the cross, God makes himself vulnerable to redeem the one he loves. Consider the following:

- Are you willing to give of yourself, both your strengths and vulnerabilities to be in a relationship?

- If we cannot maintain an intimate relationship with one who is perfect, how will we maintain a relationship with those who are not?

CHAPTER 10 – ABOUT MARRIAGE

Is Marriage the Answer?

How are Christians supposed to deal with sex? Isn't the answer to just get married? Not really. It's complicated.

I read a lot of Christian books on relationships, dating, and sex. One of the biggest faux pas the Church makes is to prescribe marriage as the answer to sexuality. Marriage is a tapestry upon which reflections of the total self, are on display through every season. Was the tapestry scorched or faded by the sun? Did it become stained? Has it become so worn it's entered winter? Everything has a season. We keep selecting partners by one season versus all seasons.

I am a woman. I'm interested in men, so I read books written by men. When you read what Christian men have written about purity you find books that stress "wait for your king." Books on marriage say, "initiate sex, lose weight, dress up, I'm being tempted everywhere I go so (woman) you'd better bring it." So it's clear we're marrying for sex. We get sex, but nothing changes for the better long term in the man or the woman. Why not?

The issue with marrying for sex is it steers you towards picking a mate who looks like a good time versus a good life. It teaches you to marry for convenience, basing the beginning of something that is supposed to be permanent on affections that are temporary. You are getting married for what you can get, rather than to build a life with someone. Your brain releases endorphins and enkephalins during intimate physical contact. You are basically drunk or high. When you come down from a high, there is a reality to deal with. When you marry for sex, you forget the requirements that come with marriage. Let me share a reality with you.

I am divorced. My brief marriage ended the year my Uncle Joe died of old age. He and my aunt were married nearly 50 years. The last 15 years were spent battling declining health from Parkinson's disease. About eight years in, it became apparent Uncle Joe would have to go into an assisted living facility. For the next seven years, my aunt would wake up in an empty bed, get up, shower, get dressed and go to the facility to spend breakfast and lunch with her husband. After lunch, she worked part-time as a church administrator then went home for dinner. She had a career in social services, but her retirement came earlier than she imagined. I won't speak to the physical intimacy of my aunt and uncle. I do know disease, as well as aging, can reduce intimacy. In the case of disease, the roaring fire of passion may morph into embers of hugs, kisses, holding hands and memories. The young, strong, handsome Harry Belafonte resemblance began drifting into the distance in time. But the fire of the expanse of their life together, I'm sure warmed her in private moments.

You don't know what life will bring you over the next 40+ years. When this person you are considering is not lying down, can they walk with you through depression, the death of your parents, disease, layoffs, miscarriages, surgeries, foreclosure, unknown children you fathered, an adoptee finding your spouse as their parent, whatever life throws at you? Can they handle success? Sex will not tell you the things true intimacy can.

Intimacy, like your faith, should be a thread that flows through every area of your relationship. Intimacy is a connection that is maintained by a series of exchanges of the core of who you are (your experiences, thoughts, hopes, fears, desires, beliefs that make up who you are) released in time to someone with whom you feel safe. This access is not granted to all. It is a private glimpse across the spectrum of who you are. You need to feel connected, accepted for who you are and safe to have intimacy. You don't need that for sex. For sex, you need body parts and a pulse. I am challenging you to be more than body parts and a pulse with a Bible. Sex in marriage requires more; more patience, more creativity, more endurance, more grace and more time. We're afraid that if someone really knew us, they wouldn't be impressed. But what a wonderful gift to be able to love someone in a way that affirms the beauty of their imperfection. When you lie in bed with your mate, you are lying next to all of their scars, their pain, their insecurities, and brokenness. You are viewing the body that stretched out and gave you intimacy, perhaps gave you children. You're looking at the frame that shouldered the burden of providing. And when these frames can no longer do these things, you don't love them less because the heart God gave you for your mate cannot relent.

The Vow is Like a Rug

One of my mentors told our group that marriage was a promise to stay with someone regardless of how they treat you. I wish I had heard about that before I got married because I would not have married. She told us that to convey marriage's permanence and how deeply you need to look into a person before you make a vow. That's like the backside of the "rug," very functional but less beautiful.

Here's the front side of the rug. The vow is a promise to never stop loving someone under any circumstances. This is where our love and God's love differs. Grace is indiscriminate. In this way, God's love is like a wanton person. God's will and his love are difficult to comprehend because it is based on himself, not anything we do. Reader, there is nothing you can do to make God fall out of love with you.

Getting to the Vow

Human love is finite. It has an end. We share a love based on who the person is, how they treat us and if we feel like loving them. At best, we evaluate the person and give them the love WE think they deserve. For the most part, we don't pick qualified, mature people, go through a godly process and make a vow to love them no matter what. I am not talking blind love. This is eyes wide open, warts and all. If you are not married, you have to be just as willing to let go of the wrong person as you are willing to hold on to the person who is right for you. We want to skip steps, but letting go of the wrong person as a single is practice for when you're married, and something looks right that's not yours. You can say "no" because you have developed that skill of saying "no." It's a part of the process. To make a good meal, you need good ingredients, a good recipe and the ability to follow directions. You will not get anything that looks like Christ and his Church with sickly ingredients, going your own way, in your sequence.

The promise to never stop loving is a heavy concept. Remember the Honor Principle? That's why the ring typically costs two month's salary. That's why the clarity and carat mean so much. That's why there is a fired metal in an infinite circle the stone is set in. It's not just jewelry. It's not just a piece of paper! It's a reflection of godly love. God is perfect. His love towards you doesn't stop. If you won't even try to keep a promise to him and remake it when you break it, how will you keep a promise to me? You're ready to *be* loved no matter what. Are you ready to *give* love no matter what?

Naked but Still Clothed

Unfortunately, not all marriages that have sex have intimacy. The following tale seems comical on one hand, but raises awareness that something else was going on.

A woman wrote to a radio show concerning intimacy in her marriage. The couple has been together for nine years. They have been married for the last three years. Everything has been wonderful. Recently the husband attended a bachelor party. After attending the bachelor party, he spent $300 on intimate apparel and accessories. Attending the bachelor party apparently awakened something in him. The wife wrote the show because her husband is now shaping the food on his dinner plate to represent private parts, and also has begun dressing up in bondage wear, chains, leather whips, etc. She comes home after a 16-hour shift to find her husband dressed in whips and chains. This resulted in an eruption of laughter. As the behavior grows more frequent, the wife becomes more distraught. She writes into the show hoping that the host can give her some advice on how to get back the man she married.[28]

When I first heard this scenario on the radio, like most people, I laughed. But as I delve more deeply, I find serious issues. On the face of what is presented, there is an obvious issue that needs attention. At first glance, it appears to me that they've been together for nine years, and she says things are "wonderful." In women's language, this means they were having sex, and she had no complaints. Then the bachelor party shows up, and now something is being offered to her that she cannot seem to gravitate toward. In plain English, before the bachelor party, they were having sex. Now, when he prepares for intimacy, she laughs at him. That's a problem. You would think he would stop and go back to what he was doing before. But there's a bigger issue here. There is a communication problem. Let's look at this from the female's point of view, with an analogy that a man can relate to.

Let's say your wife runs an errand on her lunch with a co-worker friend. She and her female friend have gone into the car dealership to get an oil change. While your wife is on the lot she happens to notice there's a sale on the new model Lexus. She hasn't had a car note for two years. The family is saving to get a new house. But she thinks because this car is on sale, she's saving you money. So she decides to go back the next day and trade her car in. You come home that evening and see a car sitting in your driveway that you don't recognize. You come in the house wondering who is visiting. There is no one there but your wife. She informs you she's just purchased a new car. How does that sit with you? Perhaps you're upset that a decision was made without you that affects you. Perhaps you feel disrespected. I imagine the wife in this scenario feels this way.

The intimacy between this husband and wife was changed without the wife's prior knowledge or consent. Their communication is at issue. How can two people be together for nine years, married for the last three years, sharing expenses, a life, physical intimacy, but are not able to talk to each other? He didn't feel comfortable about discussing this with her in advance. He made a decision about their intimacy without her input. She could not be heard by her husband, so she had to write the radio show putting me and a couple of million listeners into their business. My question is, if we can't work things out between the two of us then what do we really have?

Then I think about this from the husband's perspective. He has a good thing with his wife. He attends a bachelor party. He experiences something he thought he would like to "try at home." I give him credit because he could've wanted to try it somewhere else. Clearly, he was seeking to add excitement.

She is longing for the man she married. He is longing to share a new experience with his wife. But the beginning of that new experience needs to happen in a conversation. He could have said, "I'd like to try something new. What would you be willing to explore?" How is it that we end up sleeping next to someone we can have sex with but can't talk to?

I'm on Fire! Is Getting Married a Solution?

The previous generation of the Church believed the answer to purity was getting married based on Scripture. God said it is not good for man to be alone (Gen. 2:18). Paul said it is better to marry than to burn (I Cor. 7:9). It is best to make Christ, Lord of this area. Why? Let's examine Paul's admonition. It's better to marry than to burn. Consider a person who is burning with passion. That person is constantly trying to put their fire out. Paul suggests that instead of taking your fire to several different people, you narrow it down to one. That makes sense. It is better to stick to one person. So what's the problem with that as a solution? The problem with this scenario is the purpose of the marriage is based on YOU. It is totally supposed to meet your own desires. That is a societal standard. The Bible says that marriage is a reflection of Christ and his Church (Eph. 5: 21-23). It goes on to say; Christ gave himself for it (his bride – the Church). Let's compare this to what Adam said when he first saw Eve. "Flesh of my flesh, bone of my bone." That is not the same as, "I want you to be responsible for my lack of self-control" or "you need to make up for everything I didn't get or don't see in myself." The purpose of this type of union is to burden another person. It is dysfunctional. Where would you take your fire if the person runs into problems putting it out and re-lighting it? You're likely to take it somewhere else because you got married for your own intent. Love seeks not its own (I Cor. 13:5). You're marrying because you love your fire, not because you love the person. It is better to keep your fire to one person, but God is still expecting you to love them and do what's best for them. In this condition, are you, what's best for your intended? What are they going to get when they get you?

A View of Marriage

The ideas and images we have of being married are flawless. Gary Thomas does some myth busting in his book Sacred Marriage, with the premise, marriage is designed to make you holy more than make you happy.

> "This is a fallen world. Let me repeat this: You will never find a spouse who is not affected in some way by the reality of the Fall. If you can't respect this spouse because she is prone to certain weaknesses, you will never be able to respect any spouse."[29]

He holds up a mirror to our fallenness in conveying the ugliest dilemma of marriage. "A young bride is dismayed, horrified, full of guilt and forebodings because she is finding out little by little that she is capable of hating her husband, whom she loves faithfully. Her hatred is as real as her love. This is the reality of the human heart, the inevitability of two sinful people pledging to live together, with all their faults, for the rest of their lives."[30] This is such a relief to hear because you are shocked when you are newly married, and this happens. And it does happen. Sacred Marriage definitely separates the folks who want to *be* married from those who only want the perks of getting married.

Learning about purity is essential to marriage for at least one reason. There are some Christians who naively believe that once they meet their mate and marry, they will no longer find anyone else attractive. That is simply untrue. You are attracted to what you're attracted to. You have a type. You like what you like. If you haven't learned how to navigate that as a single person, you will not know how to deal with it as a married person. You cannot take your feet in the direction your head turns. You will find chemistry with another person besides your mate. The deal is to take your chemistry in the same direction you've already committed to. You can break the chemistry with this fleeting, temporary person. Arouse and lean into the chemistry you have with your mate. Being married means you are already committed to a partner for your chemistry project. When you study purity, you become aware of when you are bonding with someone. You learn all attention is not good attention. You learn to have accountability. These things will serve you well in marriage.

God has entrusted to you the imperfections of a person. He expects for you to be gentle and tender with all the flaws and bruised places you can see in a person. In the book of Isaiah, it is said of Jesus, "a bruised reed he will not break" (Isa. 42:3). It is Christ-like to be gentle with tender places.

I love the wedding dress shows. My favorite dresses are the bold, modern looking dresses that are ethereal but slightly distressed. They are beautifully imperfect. The imperfection is a part of the design. God is trusting you with a person. He is trusting that you will provide them a safe place to be imperfect and yet love them with grace, mercy, and tenderness in spite of their imperfections. Are you planning the wedding, the honeymoon or preparing for marriage?

Expectations of Marriage

Now Reader, this is going to sting. My expectation of marriage was consistent with a marriage myth. The myth is – the marriage is supposed to be unbreakable. The truth is that marriage is a reflected principle, displaying God's infinite love toward his people. Christ is the shining, gleaming, holy, perfect, sacrificing groom. The Church is his seriously imperfect, inconsistent, full of excuses bride. This is a match made in heaven. In a marriage between believing Christians, we both have the opportunity to imitate Christ. But this is a match made on earth between two human beings. The standard vows between these two human beings state that we "love, honor and cherish, for better or worse, in sickness and health, for richer or poorer, until death do us part." For those unmarried, we think what breaks the vow is an affair. But to break something, most of the time there has to be a crack in it first. Here's the hard part Reader, we enter marriage expecting the vows to hold. They do not hold. The vows will be broken. You need to expect them to break. Just like you drive off of the car lot with a car that's new to you, you know the tires on that car will not last for the life of the car. You buy the car knowing there will be several sets of tires in your future as long as you own the car. The vows will break. They will need to be remade. That's how marriages last.

Why do I say expect the vows to break? Look at the vow. We promised to "love, honor and cherish." Those vows alone get broken during your first really big fight (excuse me Christians – intense fellowship!). You told a minister, God and witnesses you love this person, and now you are calling them names that are seriously unlovely! Some of us have called spouses everything but a child of God! That person is *your* mate. We talk down to each other, hold grudges, etc. These things start out as small fractures, become sizeable cracks and later breaks the relationship. When the hurt spouse meets with the opportunity to get what they think they "deserve," then the sum of all of the cracks morph into broken vows. Marriages fail because the partners never expect the vow to break, so the two people are not prepared to deal with it.

So what do you do? You seal the cracks you made. You intentionally heal the places you intentionally hurt. When you do that, you remake the vow.

"Then I went down to the potter's house, and there he was, making something on the wheel. But the vessel that he was making of clay was spoiled in the hand of the potter; so he remade it into another vessel, as it pleased the potter to make."

Jeremiah 18:3-4 (NASB)

Don't you have to do that in your relationship with God? Is it really shocking you have to do that with your mate? You and your spouse will constantly be remaking the vow. That is the true nature of marriage's permanence. This is the heart of what it is to be married. This is why knowing your partner is essential before getting married. You need to select someone you will be inspired to re-commit to. These vows are a garment constantly on the mend. Sometimes life will tear it. Sometimes you will tear it. Sometimes your spouse will tear it. Sometimes your kids will tear it. And you and your spouse will constantly be mending it. In these marriages that have lasted 20, 30, 40 years, ask them how many times they had to forgive each other to stay married! The marriage can last. The vows are going to break. As they do, remake them. Take making your vow seriously. It is better not to make a vow than to make one and not fulfill it (Eccl. 5:5).

Marriage Quotes

"I believe that much of the dissatisfaction we experience in marriage comes from expecting too much from it. I have a rather outdated computer – a 486—so I know there are some things I simply can't do with it; there's just not enough memory or processing power to run certain programs or combine certain tasks. It's not that I have a bad computer, it's just that I can't reasonably expect more from it than it has the power to give.

In the same way, some of us ask too much of marriage. We want to get the largest portion of our life's fulfillment from our relationship with our spouse. That's asking too much. Yes, without a doubt there should be moments of happiness, meaning and a general sense of fulfillment. But my wife can't be God, and I was created with a spirit that craves God. Anything less than God, and I'll feel an ache." [31]

-Gary Thomas, <u>Sacred Marriage</u>

"Marriage is not the final solution to your problems. God is. Marriage is a gracious good gift from God. Proverbs 31 speaks about an excellent wife, who can find her? She does him good and not evil all the days of her life. But at the same time, if God is not at the center of your life and your mate's life, marriage creates more problems than it solves. Without the Lord at the center, marriage just brings together two self-centered people seeking self-fulfillment from one another. Put God at the center of your life. Pray that he will give you a mate with the same commitment, contentment, and godliness. Then that will bring you joy and great gain. [32]

-Bishop K. R. Woods

"People don't get married to be fixed. They get married to be loved." [33]

- Andy Stanley

"Transforming oneself in relation to one's spouse is the ultimate grindstone upon which marriage is sharpened. Each spouse is challenged to round off the rough edges and fill out the flat sides in order to make a more complete whole." [34]

-Balswick and Balswick

What Works

Dr. John Gottman studied married couples for over 25 years, noting the differences between couples who stayed happily married over the long term and those that divorced, in an attempt to save marriages. In Gottman's <u>7 Principles for Making Marriage Work</u>, he lists the behaviors successful marriages demonstrated.[35] They are:

-Learn your spouse's love map (find out what's important in their world).

-Nurture fondness and admiration (honor and respect).

-Turn toward each other (when your spouse makes a "bid" for your attention, affection, humor or support).

-Let your partner influence you (make decisions together).

-Solve your solvable problems (state feelings without blame and express positive need. Do not judge, criticize or store things up. Make and receive repair attempts).

-Overcome gridlock (unspoken, unmet expectations and goals should be addressed. Incorporate each other's goals in the marriage).

-Create a shared meaning (a family culture or way).

What Doesn't Work

Dr. Gottman also studied what doesn't work to create an antidote for it. The following are behaviors he refers to as the Four Horsemen of the Apocalypse and their counterparts:[36]

Stop these behaviors with these responses:

-Criticism – Instead use gentle start up.

-Defensiveness – Instead take responsibility for your part.

-Contempt – Instead describe your feelings. Don't describe your partner.

-Stonewalling – Instead, calm down for 20 minutes and come back to the discussion.

THINK ON THESE THINGS

When you marry, the person gets all of who you are; the way you resolve problems or let them fester, who you turn into during conflict, what you are like under pressure. There is no point hiding any of this because it will all come out. Consider the following:

-Is it really fair to blindside a person with these things?

-Are you willing to talk about how you'd both like to see these things handled?

-If marriage is the answer, what is the question?

CHAPTER 11 – PURITY PLAN

How Can I Be Pure?

I wrestled with the thought of purity. God is perfect, but I'm not. How do you undo your past? You can't un-ring a bell. It dawned on me we can only become pure, but not innocent. True innocence is not having the knowledge of/or exposure to evil. For example, porn. For people who have not seen porn (or any other form of voyeurism), they are innocent from it. The lack of seeing it is a form of protection from it. Once you've seen it, your innocence concerning this topic is gone. You cannot go back to not having seen it. Think back to the Garden of Eden when mankind was truly innocent. Now we are only made pure (not guilty) through the sacrifice of Christ. He who knew no sin (innocent), became sin (guilty) so that we could be made the righteousness of God (not guilty) in him (2 Cor. 5:21).

Purity is different from being innocent. If I were innocent, I would be led by the hand of my intended on our honeymoon night with only a vague idea of what is going to happen. But I am not innocent. Not only do I know what could happen in that room, but I also have the knowledge of my own propensities. So while I am a celibate, I, in and of myself, am not pure. The work of Christ in the life of believers makes us blameless when we were quite guilty. Our job is to remain blameless. We are not out tempting people or putting ourselves in unsafe circumstances. Not that we should live in fear, but simply possess our vessels in honor (I Thes. 4:4).

Progression

Purity is a progression. I went through four mindsets to get to this point.

-I don't want to live pure

-I can't live pure

-I don't know how to live pure

-God, help me live pure

Generally, your starting point is not wanting to live pure because you are still walking in your own way. In the second mindset, "I can't live pure," you don't see how purity is possible. You don't know you are empowered by God to live pure. This is the area where you marry for sex or live on the repentance treadmill. In the third mindset, "I don't know how to live pure," you are willing to explore purity, but you don't know how to walk it out. You may have stopped what you used to do, but you don't know what you should be doing. You know not to have sex, but you don't date at all because that's the only way you know how to stay pure. The fourth mindset, "God, help me live pure," is pursuing purity. At this point, you realize you are not your own; you are bought with a price. You also realize you cannot give yourself something God doesn't want you to have, and you trust him to provide you with God-honoring company because you won't accept anything else.

Standards and Boundaries

Who is a candidate for your company? Who is not? A question frequently asked by Christian singles is how to date non-believers. According to Scripture, we should not be unequally yoked (romantically involved) with non-believers (2 Cor. 6:14). Why not?

Dating

Let's answer that question with a question. What's your purpose in dating? In Choosing God's Best, Dr. Don Raunikar notes, "Immediate pleasure is the whole purpose for dating."[37] By and large, among Christians, we do not approach dating from a standpoint of true service. We are still looking at what's in it for us rather than determining if God is involved in this encounter. So when we lift that principle forward into marriage, the marriage does not reflect service either. If your courtship is not ministry, there's a good chance the marriage won't be either.

What service or ministry am I referring to? Let's say you meet someone who is a nonbeliever. God is drawing people to himself through you. To be Christ-centered is to have concern for others. Your motives for dealing with a nonbeliever should be to bring them to Jesus, not to yourself. Remember, God saw them first! So you've got matchless competition. The person you're attracted to may be beautiful on the outside, but they may be seriously wounded and burdened on the inside. They are looking to be loved. And love does what's best for the one it loves.

Also, keep in mind, some folks come to church to pull you out of church. When you're tempted to compromise, remember, you do not have to do anything that displeases God to get what God has for you.

Let's say you ARE dating a non-believer, but representing Christ to them. You are conducting yourself in a godly way. What happens then? One of two things will happen. Either they will begin seeking out God for themselves and genuinely be interested in having their own relationship with Jesus or they will get tired of trying to impress you with religion and tell you this is not working out.

How Do I Date You?

Let's say a man is invited to a black tie scholarship fundraiser as someone who has a social impact in the community. He meets an attractive woman and has a great conversation with her. He'd like to see her again and invites her for coffee the next day or two. He has the misfortune of living in the age of the internet. The woman has discovered he is a youth pastor. She shows up in a turtleneck and a long prairie skirt with a pocket Bible and wants to pray over the coffee. He wanted a date with the woman he met. The woman who showed up was in "junior first lady" mode[38].

Sorry Reader, I had to clear out the deep, super churchy folks and their wannabe counterparts! The first thing you do is be yourself. If you don't know who that is, you're not ready to date!

When you first meet a person, you don't know if they are a Christian or not. On the first sit down I let the man know I am a Christian. I also tell him I'm celibate. It's not something I lead with, but I get into that before the end of our meeting. I don't have a big speech about it. I come to the appointment as myself. This is who I am and how I live. I don't accept every invitation to meet. Based on my perspective, I don't go with the thought, "This could be the guy for me." I consider these initial encounters as "go see's." I'm going to see what's there. Beyond initial mutual interest and chemistry, I am asking God what's the purpose of me meeting this person. It may be just to go out and meet people. It may be something God is showing me through a person or vice versa. On my end, I'm asking God, what is the man dealing with in his life circumstances, his emotions, etc.? What condition is his life in? How, if at all, am I to help? What word am I to speak to this man? This is also what I mean by service or ministry. Service is being concerned about the needs of the person and how God will relate to them through you. God is the provider. Meeting that person's felt needs is not yours to do. But I am asking God what role am I to have in this person's story if any. I am not only talking to God about the person, but talking to God on that person's behalf.

I have removed the burden of making the date anything beyond a "go see." I am not writing my first name and his last name on a piece of paper after I meet him. The man I'm meeting can be himself. Ultimately, he belongs to God and himself; he doesn't belong to me. He is free not to be the love of my life. There is no obligation. I go with the hopes that I meet an interesting person and enjoy their company.

God can provide me with the mate he has for me because I don't want anything else. I'm not late for anything. This attitude gives us the freedom to be ourselves. I do ask questions on the date because I'm interested in him. If I weren't, I wouldn't be there.

Be willing to admit if the dating encounter is not working. It doesn't have to if it wasn't meant to. Let the interaction unfold. Allow the purpose to be revealed. You don't know why this person is sitting across from you. Pray for discernment. Be patient and let God reveal it to you. Be present in the moment rather than burdening every date you go on with the responsibility of being the fulfillment of your wildest dreams come true.

Don't put that burden on yourself or the other person.

What's your goal in dating? This will define your approach to it. If you are looking to create something long-term, you can't use short-term methods to find it.

Relational Stages

Purity looks different in different phases of your life.

Purity as a Single (Not Dating)

At this stage, purity is God being the head of your life (particularly in your romance area). The commitment to belong to him and not give away something that isn't yours (I Cor. 6:18-20). You are focused on developing your trust in God, his ways, methods, and timing. You initiate removing the partition between the two of you. Let God reveal to you the vision for your life. Develop standards, personal boundaries, deal breakers, etc.

Purity as a Single Dating

At this stage, you have found favor with someone who also has a commitment to date pure. You are the keepers of each other's purity. You are partners in agreement to serve and honor God in your frame. You wait until marriage for intercourse and any activity that starts or ends with the word "sex." A pure relationship has a goal to build a solid foundation – shared core values, getting to know your partner, learning how to fight, makeup, make decisions, communication styles as a couple, etc.

Purity as a Married Person

At this stage, you and your spouse are committed to keeping your union pure by not bringing in anything that will pollute the sweetness of your physical and emotional intimacy. You are partners in agreement to serve and honor God in your frame by being the one and only source of sexual fulfillment for each other on a continuous basis for the duration. No manipulation and no headaches! The maintenance of the relationship will include both physical and emotional intimacy, so you never lose sight of the one you love and the fulfillment of the vision you had as sweethearts.

Shopping from the Short List

"Are you a breast or a butt man?" This question was asked of a Christian single under the guise of "let's be real" on a date he was set up on in the presence of two other couples and a TV camera. So let's get real. The truth is you like what you like. Whatever parts you fancy will relocate. The body, like your car, is a depreciable asset. You are buying into something that you will struggle to maintain. When you shop from the long list, the gleam in your eye grows brighter your as daylight dims to twilight.

Test Drive

There are many people who would not marry someone they did not have sex with before marriage. So the people still deciding to wait are wondering how do you know things are compatible in bed if you don't have sex. The answer to that is simple – discernment. Funny how we only run a sex check, but not a health test, credit check, background check and a holiness check. The Holy Spirit can reveal things to you if you allow yourself to be Spirit-led. Let me give you some examples.

Let's say when you go out to dinner; you like to try dishes you normally don't make at home. You are dating someone who refuses to sample anything they don't already eat. They normally eat chicken, but once they find out Marsala is wine, and there's a mushroom involved, chicken Marsala is off the menu. I'm not saying you have to like it, but some people won't even try. Some folks need to have things in an exact way. They're wound up super tight. There are also people who are on the date and on the phone for extended periods of time. Others may be highly critical. I saw a comedy show where a man in his late twenties got a ride from his mother to have a midnight rendezvous. This man made no effort to get to the woman on his own. How much effort was he going put into sexual activity?

Would you really want that in bed with you? If your perspective of sex is an uninhibited experience, you cannot create that with someone who's super picky, hypercritical and unwilling to consider anything new. And laziness is not acceptable under any circumstances. All of these traits have the potential to end up in bed with you.

Keep in mind, without an intervening factor (counseling, journaling, mentorship, the Holy Spirit) working in someone's life, the nature of a person doesn't change. Perfect (mature; well developed) love, casts out fear (I John 4:18). Fear is something you don't want in bed with you. Your past is something you don't want in bed with you.

How Far Can I Go?

Think of the characteristics that demonstrate love to you – loyalty, encouragement, honesty, someone who would protect you, look out for you and have your back. Tie your virtues to your boundaries. For example, I have made a dating boundary that I will not kiss a man I don't know. I think affection is appropriate in dating. I just want to save my lip lock for a man I know. That makes the focus of dating getting to know each other rather than getting a kiss. Of course over time, one will catch up with the other, and you'll be getting to know a person and getting kissed.

No, Really, How Far Can I Go?

We have a little sister, and her breasts are not yet grown. What shall we do for our sister on the day she is spoken for? If she is a wall, we will build towers of silver on her. If she is a door, we will enclose her with panels of cedar.

Song of Solomon 8:8-10 (NIV)

Are you a wall or are you a door? You can't walk through a wall, but anyone can walk through a door. Personal boundaries will vary by individual. I attended a wedding between two believers who were 50+. They mutually agreed to have their first kiss at the altar on their wedding day. I applauded them, but I don't know if I could do that. The first kiss and the consummation all in one day would be a lot for me. So what can you do?

I can speak a lot about religion here, but I know what you want to know is something along the lines of, "Let's say I know them after some time. Can I put my hands on my sweetheart's butt?" If you're looking for someone to tell you it's OK to sit on a sofa and play a game of "find the remote" by petting each other and telling God you're sorry, you won't get that from me. You are accountable to God for your own behavior. Here's the deal. The purpose of that action is to get a reaction, a spark, to start a fire that will need to be quenched. A lot of believers end up falling because they think sex will take them from date to mate. People who come to you for sex usually don't stay for marriage. This may occur in rare cases. However, do you think God would send you someone who would lead you in a direction opposite to his Word? Remember, you are not shopping for the night time you are shopping for a lifetime.

In the meantime, let's look at much more practical information. Desmond Morris, a behavioral scientist, identified 12 steps of intimacy which provide us the opportunity to think before we act.[39] Where will you draw your line?

-Eye to Body

-Eye to Eye

-Voice to Voice

-Hand to Hand

-Hand to Shoulder

-Hand to Waist

-Face to Face

-Hand to Head

-Hand to Body

-Mouth to Body

-Touching Below the Waist

-Intercourse

Pursuing Purity

> Now in a large house there are not only gold and silver vessels, but also vessels of wood and of earthenware, and some to honor and some to dishonor. Therefore, if anyone cleanses himself from these things, he will be a vessel for honor, sanctified, useful to the Master, prepared for every good work. Now flee from youthful lusts and pursue righteousness, faith, love and peace, with those who call on the Lord from a pure heart.
>
> 2 Timothy 2:20-22 (NASB)

Purity must be pursued to be maintained. Think of it as a chase scene. You are chasing purity. Temptation is chasing you. When you stop, purity is shrinking far from your sight and temptation is at your heels.

Maintaining Purity

Flee youthful lust. Instead, pursue righteousness with those who call on the name of the Lord out of a pure heart. Based on this passage of Scripture, I believe a group that studies relationships is better than studying alone. In group, we studied some aspect of these principles quarterly. Faith comes by hearing. This implies a perpetual process.

THINK ON THESE THINGS

We know the Bible describes sexual intercourse as "one flesh." Consider the following:

-Where is the beginning of "one flesh?"

-How far can you go and still be godly?

-What boundaries will you and your partner set?

-Where are you going to draw the line?

CHAPTER 12 – MAINTENANCE PLAN

As you are driving your car, the gas pump icon glows red on your dashboard. This is a warning light. There is another button you can tap that will tell you how many miles you can drive until your gas tank is empty. One of the relationship questions I ask is, "What's your maintenance plan?" What are the relational lights that indicate you are running low in an important area that if left un-serviced, the relationship will break down and eventually stop?

We start relationships without thinking about how to maintain them. What do I mean? We purchase a car knowing it will break down. We've already considered the maintenance. Yet we date or marry without ever considering there will be a breakdown. We act like the people we love will never offend us, as if they are not supposed to. We never consider that we may offend them. It is a very naïve thought based on our track record. A neglected car is going to cost you a lot. A neglected relationship will cost even more.

One of the questions I ask when I date is, "What are you like when you get angry or offended?" The man will always tell me he's a great communicator and likes to talk things out. That is not who shows up in the relationship. What I usually encounter is willfulness, tantrums or someone who tries to verbally bully. Many times the irony is the person doesn't know that's who they will turn into. They think because I'm here, it will be different. I may react differently than what they're used to, but they have not yet learned how to handle their emotions.

The relationship is the vehicle the two individual people are sitting in. When you bring these challenges into the relationship without any maintenance plan, the car breaks down and runs out of gas. This is why some of the relationships only go so far. If you have no plan to deal with disagreements, then your plan is for your partner not to make you mad. So what are you going to do when life happens?

Borrowing from Gary Chapman's book <u>The Five Love Languages</u>, let's say love is quality time. How long can you go without quality time before you would consider it a relational problem (in the red)? How many attempts to raise the issue (the dashboard light coming on) do you think would be sufficient to get a response?

THINK ON THESE THINGS

Contrast the maintenance with your posture from the beginning. When we start out dating, we have such deep devotion. Every moment together is important. We are offering our time, devotion and eventually our singleness to concentrate on the one in whom our affections rest. We pay a price of being vulnerable and are open to being loved. Yet once we have this partner, we can sacrifice this same person because over time, winning the argument means more. The maintenance plan is simply this – you will either maintenance your relationship or your ego. You cannot do both. Are you willing to give of yourself to keep a mate or just to get a mate?

CHAPTER 13 - VISION

Where there is no vision, the people perish.

Proverbs 29:18 (KJV)

Vision is the lynchpin that holds me in place. It is the reason I don't settle. I have a fixed picture in my mind of the home I want to share with my mate. How we will work and play together, the harmony of our home. We will both be excited to come home. I have a set idea of how we will speak with each other in private as well as in public. I have a firm picture of the type of leader the man will be and my respect for him. The vision weeds out those who are immature or ill-prepared for the level of commitment I have to offer.

You cannot have a clear picture of your future if you are still stuck in your past. Christ being handled by Thomas after the resurrection was ministry on one of its most intimate levels (John 20:24-16). For Thomas to handle Jesus' wounds, they had to be healed. Otherwise, Jesus would have reacted in pain. Can you imagine what being healed from your past looks like? Can you imagine being respected or being important to another person? What would someone befriending you look like?

Now that you know about a purity plan and your maintenance plan, what do they look like in your vision? Can you see someone willing to wait and getting to know you? Can you see yourself dating and making the date about foundational things instead of temporary things? Can you see the two of you talking your problems out, ganging up on the problem instead of each other? Can you see each other apologizing? Can you see a friend in this person? What's your vision? As a man thinks in his heart, so is he (Prov. 23:7).

THINK ON THESE THINGS

What's the difference between fantasy and vision? The purpose of fantasy is distraction. The purpose of vision is fulfillment. Pretending you're never going to argue (fantasy) is not the same as having a vision of working out your problems, then taking courses to learn about communication and conflict resolution. Consider the following:

- What do you need to receive to experience fulfillment in your relationships?

- What do you need to work on to become the person you envision?

CHAPTER 14 - RESOLUTION

Love TBD

I found you lying there in pieces.
Nothing but body parts
Strewn together for pleasure
For private endeavors
None of which led to
Knowing you any better.
I barely knew your name,
If you had a brain,
And what you wanted to be
When you grew up at five years old.
But truth be told
I'm sure it wasn't being
My plaything.
Yet I'm here playing games with you
Asking sensuous rhetorical questions
Whose answers feel good.
Another life test
We keep failing.
A sexpert with
A remedial knowledge of love.
Love is so big
If we were really
Walking with it
Between our legs
We wouldn't get far
Because we'd trip over it.
And we do trip over it.
Love is the one partner
We refuse to enter fully into.
It strips us of our pride
Then viewing every imperfection
Washes us in truth
Holds us in grace
Clothes us in humility
Because we have done nothing

To deserve so great a gift.
Maybe we didn't know how to treat it.
Are you accusing love
For not being love?
Love on trial
And you lose.
If you were on trial for
Loving someone
Would there be a scratch or a bruise
On your heart to prove
You went beyond your heart
Convicted by the love you feared to lose?
Or would they find you had an alibi
Because your heart
Was not at home?
Would your body tell the lie
That you were present
But you left love's heart alone?
If you were on trial for love
Is there enough evidence
For you to be convicted?
Or did you take the safe way out
The safest route
And stand at a distance
Because you were too
Conflicted?
You stood by as love
Went its way and
Pretended it never visited.
We are not angry because love
Never came.
We are angry because it
Didn't stay as long as
The longing we had for it.
We stand bereft of love,
Leaving on our lips
The echo of love's name.
Rather than get ready to love,
We take revenge on love
And reduce it to a stain.
Seducing those who came
Close enough to entertain
Our attention and chase away

Our loneliness for a little while.
Looking back at our conquests
We smile a crooked smile
Keeping at bay
The cracks in our hearts.
And I am mocked
Because I'd rather
Love in whole
Than in part.
I'd rather stay outside
The norm than fit in.
Readily I admit my chiefest sin
Is that when love shows up
I'm afraid to go in.
But I have learned
Love has no fools
Only brave souls
Who had more love than
The object of its affection
Could receive.
Love only returns to hearts
That believe.
Love me unpolished
Imperfect
And raw
Love me completely
Or not at all.

I respect love,
Enough to be
Worthy of it.
I embrace
The gift of love,
Enough to
Have the courage
To open it.
I receive love,
Enough to
Open up
For it.
When I see love
I will welcome it.
Like the sun in winter,

Like the wind
In September,
Like a spring thaw
Or summer harvest,
I will Marvel
In every season.
I am love's
Inspiration,
Devotion,
I am its reason.
I give love
My full
Attention.
I give love
Its introspection.
I give love
The depth
It is seeking.
With eyes
Roaming,
To and fro,
To and fro,
To and fro
To show its heart
Strong in love,
Weak in self-seeking.
I bind love's wounds
When its heart
Is bleeding.
I am by love's side
When its heart turns pale
And stops beating.
Laid hands on Love
Willing it back to life.
Duality in one being.
I am Love's mistress.
I am Love's wife.
Both passion and home
Roam step for step,
Age to age.
Nursing at the cradle.
Cradle at the grave.
I have love

And love has me.
High as the heavens,
Deep as the seas.
As the roar whispers,
Wind tickle in the breeze.
I invest this one life for
Love to do
What it wants with me.

-D. Horne, 2015

Purity is a reflection of your relationship with God. I describe my relationship with God in the following analogy. God and I are like an old married couple. We look cozy now, but we've had bumps in the beginning. It's as if my life is a car. I ran my car into a ditch, and God comes along to help push the car out of the ditch. After getting out of the ditch, I let God drive. We start riding along God and I. Then, I don't like where God is taking me. God and I argue. I am clearly right. To make God see how right I am, I hop out of the car. You don't really know if you have a solid bond with someone until you've gotten mad and fallen out with them, and God is no exception. God starts driving slow following me along the road as I'm walking, trying to get me to get back in the car. He talks me back into the car. I get in, but I try to push him out of the driver's seat and take the wheel again. I end up in the trunk. I decide to make up with God. I recommit to being a partner with God on our journey through life together rather than thinking of God as my probation officer and myself as one of his parolees. Now I'm a co-pilot because I've accepted the course God has charted. Good thing got me trained while we were in the car on the ground!

I tell you this scenario Reader so you know that living for God is something you can do. Many times people come to faith thinking that they have to be "perfect" or syrupy sweet and super religious. Jesus comes in grace and truth so you might as well stop looking for a personality transplant and be yourself (John 1:14,17). God can meet you where you are. So like it or not, your purity is a reflection of your trust in God and his role in your life.

Stained

During communion, I dipped the wafer in the cup. The wafer became stained. I begin thinking of those television crime shows where they are looking for evidence of the crime. Many times the assailant has washed and scrubbed the crime scene. The investigators bring a substance called luminal. They spray the scene, turn off the light and shine a black light on it. The chemicals in the blood react to the luminal. An area that previously looked clean turns blue. In spite of appearances, the blood still speaks. If you have received Jesus as Savior and Lord, you were cleansed by his blood for the remission of your sins (Heb. 9:11-19). When a garment is dyed, the color of the garment is permanently changed. We have the blood, but we need to keep the stain of it instead of trying to wash it away.

"Should sin abound so grace may much more abound? God forbid" (Rom. 6:1-2). We belong to God. We read Scripture, but we need to let Scripture read us. We have faith, but we need to let faith have us.

Sacrifice

According to Romans 12:1, we are to present our bodies as a living sacrifice. This living sacrifice phrase conveys a process. A sacrifice is when something living must be killed. So the will, the desires of the flesh, must constantly be killed. Fortunately for us, God's mercies are new every morning (Lam. 3:23).

Our flesh has its own inclinations. It wants to sleep 5 minutes longer that it should. It wants another bowl of ice cream. It struggles to exercise. Think of our relationship with our flesh as a large dog we are walking. Some days we are walking the dog and the dog is going where we are walking. Other days, the dog is pulling us somewhere, and we need to rein it in. Galatians compares the works of the flesh vs. the fruit of the Spirit.

So I say, walk by the Spirit, and you will not gratify the desires of the flesh. For the flesh desires what is contrary to the Spirit, and the Spirit what is contrary to the flesh. They are in conflict with each other so that you are not to do whatever you want. But if you are led by the Spirit, you are not under the law.

The acts of the flesh are obvious: sexual immorality, impurity, and debauchery; idolatry and witchcraft; hatred, discord, jealousy, fits of rage, selfish ambition, dissensions, factions, and envy; drunkenness, orgies, and the like. I warn you, as I did before, that those who live like this will not inherit the kingdom of God.

But the fruit of the Spirit is love, joy, peace, forbearance, kindness, goodness, faithfulness, gentleness, and self-control. Against such things, there is no law. Those who belong to Christ Jesus have crucified the flesh with its passions and desires. Since we live by the Spirit, let us keep in step with the Spirit.

Galatians 5:16-25 (NIV)

How does this work? Imagine you are in a room at night with the lights off. When you turn the light on darkness leaves. As long as that light is on, darkness cannot come in. But if you turn that light out, darkness will return. Walking in the Spirit is like the light being on in that room. If you do not walk in the Spirit, you will walk in the flesh. Turning the light on is your choice. You don't get to pick the situation life hands you, but you can make a choice how to react to it and how to deal with it. Galatians shows the fruit of the fleshly, selfish thinking. Let's look at the opposite, love.

Love is patient; love is kind. It does not envy, it does not boast, it is not proud. It does not dishonor others, it is not self-seeking, it is not easily angered, it keeps no record of wrongs. Love does not delight in evil but rejoices with the truth. It always protects, always trusts, always hopes, always perseveres. Love never fails.

I Corinthians 13:4-8 (NIV)

If you do not see these attributes in a person, then they do not have love. These are the thoughts and actions of love. In reading this passage, it is clear to me the opposite of love is not necessarily lust but selfishness. I've taken liberties here to demonstrate my meaning more clearly. I have set this passage in the opposite to the original text.

4 Selfishness is impatient; selfishness is unkind. It envies, it boasts, it is proud.

5 It dishonors others; it is self-seeking, it is easily angered, it keeps a record of wrongs and holds grudges.

6 Selfishness delights in evil (celebrating the hard times of others); it evades (runs from) the truth.

7 It always exposes and blames, always distrusts, always despairs and is fearful, gives up easily and never completes anything.

8 Selfishness is never satisfied.

Love is a fruit of the Spirit. Anything opposite of love is a work of the flesh. Remember that light analogy? If you don't set your default attitude to attributes of love, you are likely to walk in selfishness and flesh. These are the attitudes that do not reflect God and must be sacrificed. This is what it means to "die to self."

Transformation

Romans 12:2 says we are transformed by the renewing of our minds. An example of that would be your friend is getting married, and you are experiencing envy. You go through the concordance of the Bible and read all the passages on envy. You get to the root of the envy. It's not that you believe your friend doesn't deserve their happiness. You feel the pressure of your desire for a mate and the weight of your current singleness. The friend's upcoming wedding intensifies this weight. Envy is lying to you. God blessing your friend has nothing to do with you. God did not give them a mate to make you feel bad. God doesn't love your friend more than he loves you. He loves us all the same. Envy is telling you something about God that is not true. This is why you need to study Scripture. God's character is revealed in his Word. So when envy tells you things about God that are not true, you know not to keep feeding that thought and to start meditating on the truth of who God is. Left unaddressed, this thought could grow into a desperate action from hooking up with an old flame just to have someone, to bitterness ruining your friendship. Thoughts turn into action.

I would encourage you to have a frank conversation with God about it. If you feel God is late, tell him that. If you feel slighted, tell him that. This is still prayer. This is a part of your relationship with him. God is a big God. He can handle it. You will need to create a quiet block of time to hear from God. In this instance, you will likely wrestle between two truths. One, God is a provider. He has promised to supply all your need (Phil. 4:19). He is not bound by your circumstance. He has all the resources necessary to meet your need. Two, God works his will on his schedule, not ours. You may feel helpless. Instead of being locked into what you can't have or do, think about what you can do. You can get prepared for what you are asking God for. You can also expand the circles you travel in. If you focus your prayers on asking God for illumination in those two areas, you may find the ability to celebrate your friend's wedding with the right attitude. Renewing your mind is looking at things with a godly perspective. Renewing your mind includes the Word, prayer and godly counsel.

Next Steps

Invite God into this area. Most people think they're doing this when they feel guilty about a thought, behavior or situation and repent. But that's not what I'm talking about. I'm talking about going before God with this area of your life, surrendering it and asking him what you can do to improve it. "God, this is not an area I feel I'm progressing in. How can I make this aspect of my life better? How can I make it healthy? How can I make it strong? I want to quit being embarrassed by it or stop crying over it. I'd like a better outcome."

Get A Fuller Vision for This Area of Your Life

When it comes to romance, we stop at fantasy and don't push it all the way to vision. You should have a vision for your life with a mate. What is the level you're living on? What is the atmosphere of your home life?

What do you want people to say when they look at how you and your mate interact? What would you want other people to say about your mate? What kind of temperament do they have? Fill in the blanks.

Get Real About This Season in Your Life

What is the actual infrastructure of your world and how would a person fit into it? Consider how a dating life would look different if you're taking care of an aged parent, pursuing an advanced degree or a single parent with small children. Do you have time to date? Can you balance time for yourself, time for your kids, time for your friends, time for work, time for God and time for this person? If you're not sure, ask God what's the priority for this season in your life.

Reconciliation

Adam naming his wife Eve (mother of all living), is a point of forgiveness and reconciliation. Through Christ, we have the ministry of reconciliation (2 Cor. 5:18). We must reconcile the broken, hurting self to the new life in Christ. As we make efforts on that front, we begin to serve with authenticity and understand others. The greatest commandment states, "You must love the Lord your God with all your heart, mind, soul and strength and love your neighbor as yourself" (Deut. 6:5; Luke 10:27).

The Bottom Line

I have shown you the pertinent pieces of this puzzle of purity. The biggest piece is your decision to live *for* God out of your relationship *with* God. Your research, study, discussion and application of the principles must be constant. It is the only way to make them a part of how you live. You will revisit how you are to be loved, belong and matter throughout your life span. Make sure the conversation you start with God continues.

Epilogue

This book is about how to apply Scripture to follow Christ in the area of romantic relationships. You have seen by now the way to do that is to improve your view of God, sex, relationships, yourself and others. For too long we church people have lived however we wanted romantically and asked God to bless those relationships and/or forgive us. Some with opposite gendered people. Some with same-gendered people. Some with available people. Some with people that availed themselves to several people and some with unavailable people. The message of the gospel of Jesus Christ is grace. It is universally available to all who seek it.

"For God so loved the world that he gave his one and only Son, that whoever believes in him shall not perish but have eternal life. For God did not send his Son into the world to condemn the world, but to save the world through him."

John 3:16 - 17 (NIV)

May God give us all the grace to live in his truth and save us to the uttermost.

In His Service,

Danielle Horne

PURITY RESOURCES

To continue your journey, pick up more resources on purity and connect with Danielle at:

Website: www.purityinprogress.com

Facebook: www.facebook.com/PurityinProgress

Twitter: @MsDHorneSpeaks

Instagram: @MsDHorneSpeaks

Email: msdhornespeaks@yahoo.com

Address: Danielle Horne
                C/O Black Rim Media & Publishing
                1480 Moraga Rd., Suite C #231
                Moraga, CA 94556

END NOTES

Chapter 1 - The Playbook

[1] Andy Stanley, <u>Visioneering: God's Blueprint for Developing and Maintaining Vision,</u> Colorado Springs, CO, Multnomah Books, 1999. 63. Print.

Chapter 2 - About God

[2] Gary L. Thomas, <u>Sacred Marriage: What If God Designed Marriage to Make Us Holy More Than to Make Us Happy?</u> Grand Rapids, MI, Zondervan, 2000. 108-109. Print.

[3] John W. Stott, <u>The Radical Disciple: Some Neglected Aspects of Our Calling,</u> Downers Grove, IL, IVP Books, InterVarsity Press, 2010, 99 and Preface. Print.

[4] Stott, pp. 15 – 16.

Chapter 3 - About You

[5] Olivia. DifferenceBetween.com. "Difference Between Expression and Equation." N.P., 17 February 2011. Web. 24 Aug. 2016. http://www.differencebetween.com/difference-between-expression-and-vs-equation/

[6] ThinkExist.com Quotations. "William J. Toms quotes". <u>ThinkExist.com Quotations Online</u> 1 Dec. 2016. 23 Dec. 2015 http://en.thinkexist.com/quotes/william_j._toms/

[7] *BibleGateway.com.* www.BibleGateway.com, 1 May 15. Web. 9 May 15 https://www.biblegateway.com/passage/?search=Genesis%2026:8,&version=DRA

[8] Dallying (def. 2) "dally". <u>Dictionary.com Unabridged</u>. Random House, Inc. 9 May 2015. Dictionary.com http://dictionary.reference.com/browse/dally

[9] *BibleGateway.com.* www.BibleGateway.com, 1 May 15. Web. 9 May 15 https://www.biblegateway.com/passage/?search=Genesis%2026:8,&version=DARBY

[10] Joseph S. Exell and Henry D. M. Spence-Jones. "Commentary on Genesis 26:8."

Studylight.org. The Pulpit Commentary, 1 May 15. Web. 9 May 15.
http://www.studylight.org/commentaries/tpc/view.cgi?bk=ge&ch=26

[11] Rob Hill, Sr. For Single People Who Still Understand The Value of
Relationships. Chesapeake, VA: Spirit Filled Creations, 2012. 59. Print.

[12] "sternal rib." The American Heritage® Medical Dictionary. 2007. Houghton
Mifflin Company 22 Dec. 2015 http://medical-
dictionary.thefreedictionary.com/sternal+rib

Chapter 5 - About Your Body

[13] David Eckman, Sex, Food, & God. Eugene, Or.: Harvest House, 2006. 47. Print.

Chapter 6 - About Temptation

[14] Nancy Groom, Risking Intimacy: Overcoming Fear, Finding Rest. Grand Rapids,
MI: Baker, 2000. 128. Print.

Chapter 7 - About Honor

[15] James Strong, "Kabad or Kabed." BibleHub.com. Strong's Exhaustive
Concordance of the Bible, 1 Jan. 2015. Web. 31 Jan. 2015.
http://biblehub.com/hebrew/3513.htm

[16] Robert L. Thomas, "Kabad or Kabed." BibleHub.com. New American Standard
Exhaustive Concordance of the Bible, 1 Jan. 2015. Web. 31 Jan. 2015.
http://biblehub.com/hebrew/3513.htm

[17] George V. Wigram, "Timios." BibleHub.com. Englishman's Greek Concordance of
the New Testament, 1 Jan. 2015. Web. 31 Jan. 2015
http://biblehub.com/greek/timios_5093.htm

Chapter 8 – About Sex

[18] Helen Fisher, PH.D. "What's Love Got to Do with It? Intimacy: His & Hers." O
The Oprah Magazine, October (2009): 138. Web 22 Dec. 2015
http://www.helenfisher.com/downloads/articles/Oprah_1009.pdf

[19] Maria Popova, "This Is Your Brain on Love." Brain Pickings. N.P., 11 June
2010. Web. 30 Nov. 2014. https://www.brainpickings.org/2010/06/11/your-
brain-on-love/

[20] "Euphoria." *Merriam-Webster.com*. Merriam-Webster, N.D. Web. 30 Nov. 2014.

[21]"licentious." American Heritage® Dictionary of the English Language, Fifth Edition. 2011. Houghton Mifflin Harcourt Publishing Company 12 May 2015 http://www.thefreedictionary.com/licentious

[22] Rick Stedman, Your Single Treasure: The Good News about Singles and Sexuality. Chicago: Moody, 2000. 96-97. Print.

[23] Stedman. 91-92.

[24] Gary L. Thomas, Sacred Marriage: What If God Designed Marriage to Make Us Holy More Than to Make Us Happy? Grand Rapids, MI, Zondervan, 2000. 221. Print.

[25] The Count of Monte Cristo. Dir. Kevin Reynolds. Perf. James Caviezel, Guy Pearce, Richard Harris, James Frain, Dagmara Dominczyk and Luis Guzman. Buena Vista Pictures, 2002. DVD.

[26]"rape." American Heritage® Dictionary of the English Language, Fifth Edition. 2011. Houghton Mifflin Harcourt Publishing Company 23 Dec. 2015 http://www.thefreedictionary.com/rape

[27] Villa Teen Apprentices. "Seduction in Ancient Rome." The Getty Iris. The J. Paul Getty Trust, 12 Apr. 13. Web. 23 Dec. 2015. http://blogs.getty.edu/iris/seduction-in-ancient-rome/

Chapter 10 – About Marriage

[28] "Strawberry Letter- A Disrespectful Husband!" WDAS. Steve Harvey in the Morning, 2 Nov. 13. Web. 9 May. 2015. http://www.wdasfm.com/onair/steve-harvey-in-the-morning-21957/strawberry-letter-a-disrespectful-husband-11675458/

[29] Gary L. Thomas, Sacred Marriage: What If God Designed Marriage to Make Us Holy More Than to Make Us Happy? Grand Rapids, MI, Zondervan, 2000. 69. Print.

[30] Gary L. Thomas, 15 -16.

[31] Gary L. Thomas, 25-26.

[32] K. R. Woods, Love Sex & Relationship Trilogy, Successful Single Living, K. R. Woods Ministries, 2 Mar. 2015. CD.

[33] Andy Stanley, <u>The New Rules for Love, Sex and Dating</u>, Grand Rapids, MI, Zondervan, 2011. 62. Print.

[34] Judith K. Balswick and Jack O. Balswick, <u>Authentic Human Sexuality: An Integrated Christian Approach</u>. Downers Grove, IL: InterVarsity, 1999. 148-49. Print.

[35] John Mordechai Gottman and Nan Silver. <u>The Seven Principles for Making Marriage Work</u>. New York: Crown, 1999. Print.

[36] Gottman and Silver. 27-33.

Chapter 11 – Purity Plan

[37] Don Raunikar, <u>Choosing God's Best: Wisdom for Lifelong Romance</u>. Sisters, Or.: Multnomah, 1998. 21. Print.

[38] Niema Jordan, "Praying for Love." <u>Essence</u> July 2009: 80. Print.

[39] Desmond Morris, <u>Intimate Behaviour.</u> New York: Random House, 1972. 74-78. Print.

www.ingramcontent.com/pod-product-compliance
Lightning Source LLC
Chambersburg PA
CBHW051816040426
42446CB00007B/704